T0117043

I'm Not Going Mad, I'm Just Coming Into Myself, After Living Through Dying Places

J'Korey Mills

iUniverse, Inc.
Bloomington

I'm Not Going Mad, I'm Just Coming Into Myself, After Living Through Dying Places

iUniverse books may be ordered through booksellers or by contacting:

iUniverse
1663 Liberty Drive
Bloomington, IN 47403
www.iuniverse.com
1-800-Authors (1-800-288-4677)

ISBN: 978-1-4620-0018-0 (sc)
ISBN: 978-1-4620-0019-7 (ebk)

Printed in the United States of America

iUniverse rev. date: 3/8/2011

THE YEAR OF THE LORDS FAVOR!
(Isaiah 61:1-11)

The Spirit of the Sovereign Lord is on me, because the Lord has anointed me, to preach the good news to the poor. He has sent me to bind up the brokenhearted, to proclaim freedom from the captives and release from darkness for the prisoners, to proclaim of the year of the Lords Favor and the day of vengeance of our God, to comfort all who mourn, and provide for those who grieve in Zion, to bestow on them a crown of beauty instead of ashes, the oil of gladness instead of mourning, and a garment of praise instead of a spirit of despair. They will be called oaks of righteousness, a planting of the Lord for the display of his splendor. They will rebuild the ancient ruins and destroy the places long devastated; they will renew the ruined cities that have been devastated for generations. Aliens will shepherd your flocks; foreigners will work your fields and vineyards. And you will be called priest of the Lord, you will be named ministers of our God. You will feed on the wealth of nations, and in their riches you will boast. Instead of their shame, my people will receive a double portion, and instead of disgrace they will rejoice in their inheritance; and so they will inherit a double portion in their land, and everlasting joys will be theirs. (8vs) **"For I, the Lord, love justice; I hate robbery and iniquity. In my faithfulness I will reward them and make an everlasting covenant with them. Their descendants will be known among the nations and their offspring's among the peoples. All who** see them will acknowledge that they are people of the **Lord has blessed."** I delight greatly in the Lord; my soul rejoices in my God. for he has clothe me with garments of salvation and arrayed me in a robe of righteousness, as a bridegroom adorns his head like a priest, and as a bride adorns herself with her jewels. For as the soil makes the sprout come up and a garden causes seeds to grow, so the Sovereign Lord will make righteousness and praise spring up before all nations.

61:8 Key Point: We suffer for many reasons-our ways, mistakes, someone else's mistakes, injustice. When we suffer from our own mistakes, we get what we deserve. When we suffer because of others or because of injustice, God is angry. God in his mercy says that his people have suffered enough. God will reward those who suffer because of injustice, He will settle all accounts.

ACKNOWLEDGMENTS

First giving honor to Jehovah Jireh, God whom is my provider. Jehovah Nissi, God whom is my banner. Jehovah Shiloh, God whom is my peace. I want to thank him for the gifts that he has given me to Minister to others through writing, and for letting me know that I'll understand it better by and by. I want to give Extravagant Praise to him for allowing me to write this book. For the battle is not mine, it belongs to the Lords.

I want to give a sincere thanks to Pastor Alexander D Hurt for his phenomenal teachings. I want him to know that "My Harvest Is Living In Fullness Now, Visioning Plays A Important Role In My Life, My World Is Now Framed With my Words, I Have Prevailed In Prayer To See Results in The Earth, I Now Know How Extravagant God Is And How He Over Does More Than We Expect, Flesh Fights, Five Signs Of A Growing Believer, Holiness, And Finally The Third Birth. I want him to know, that after all the years of growing up in the church as a child I have never experienced a new level in Christ until I sat under his teachings. I want to thank him for the time he met with me in his office and allowed me to express to him the calling that God had upon my life. And for prophesying what God had spoken unto him, to say to me **"Humble Yourselves, Therefore, Under God's Mighty Hand, That He May Lift You Up In Due Time"** (1st Peter Chapter 5, verse 6) As Pastor Hurt said be careful of faucets that call themselves the source, and to guard your heart and mind against negative spirits. Thank You Pastor Alexander D Hurt and May God continue to bless you and Missionary Ty Hurt, and the Hurt Household as well as the Kingdom Church Family of Brockton Ma.

Thank You Bishop Eddie Long and The New Birth Choir, for Ministering to me through song and the word of God That were spoken by Bishop Long, " He said the day is over for you to keep quiet, people being upset about your dreams , because you are talking about stuff that has not even happen, that's about to happen. Being exposed in the light of God, any moment and day and any time I'm about to manifest and bless somebody. I'm about to be ordained in the sight of God, "oh, oh, oh" bam the lights are going to hit me. I'm just in the dark room being processed.

Thank You Kurt Carr for "God Blocked It", and Tremaine Hawkins for a "Change Has Come over Me. Dorinda Clark Cole for "That's The Reason" Vickie Winans for "Shake Your Self Loose" Dr. Charles Hayes and The Cosmopolitain Mass Choir "Jesus Can Work It out Part One" Dianne Williams, words can't describe the blessing that God Has upon Your Life. You have out done your self with "Jesus Can Work It out Remix" Girl I have had to jump out the car on numerous occasions and act a fool in the middle of the street, because I felt your spirit piercing through the speakers of my car. You have a true testimony that I can somewhat relate too. Thank You!!

To my friend Noel Rainford, I truly thank you, if it was not for you and the grace of God; I would not have been able to write this book. Not only was I your paper carrier, but a workout partner as well, and who would have ever thought that you would end up taking on a paper route, God has truly blessed you with a beautiful family. God Bless!!! That goes to show you that you will never know, where your next blessing is going to come from.

I truly want to thank all of who was there for me in the time of famine, it is so true that God has a way of showing us the real side of our friends and family, because in the time when I had plenty and was doing well, everyone had their hand out looking for something, or speaking negative words against me, and in my time of famine none of you could be found.

The late Dr. Bishop Joe L. Smith once said "Nothing In, Nothing Out, Something In, and Something Out, Nothing for Nothing Leaves Nothing"

To all the former and present staff ; at The Home for Little Wanderers, Edna Stein Academy (which is no longer in existence) , Fall River Diagnostic Assessment Center, and The Growing Minds Resource Institute (who is also no longer in existence), and the Department of Social Services Thank You!!!

To all those who said I would not amount to anything and looked down on me and talked about me like a dog, I'm here to tell you that I made it, not by your grace, but by God's grace, because he created me in his own image and likeness, favor is not fair, but it is necessary in the sight of God. He saw the best in me when every one else around could only see the worst in me, as Pastor Hurt said "I'm not better than you, I'm just above you"

Finally I want to thank Whitney Houston for, I didn't know my own strength, and I know that I was not built to break, even though I crashed down, and stumbled, but I did not crumble, and I got through all the pain, and I'm glad to say, I got to know my own strength, because I truly was not, In Jesus Name, Built To Break!!!!!!

Prologue

This book is meant to Minister to those who have, or is dealing with the same issues that I have been dealing with for all these years and holding in the pain that no one knows but you and Daddy God. I have been called to tell my story and I am not ashamed to finally open up and tell the truth. God knew this day was going too come before I did, and what I went through did not catch him by surprise. God is the only one that can turn a Mess into a Message, and a Test into a Testimony, and a Trial into Triumph, and give the Victim the Victory. For we've been made to endure for a night, but always remember joy will come in the morning. Morning does not mean am or pm; it is when God calls you out of darkness, into his marvelous light.

I hope and pray that this book touches many lives, especially to the youth who are the next generation to come. Often times we hear our parents say "I've been in this world a lot longer than you". So that you know, that raises a red flag with me, because yes our parents may have been in the world, but the key point is, are they in Christ? Because the bible teaches them to raise a child in the way that they should go, so that when he or she grows old they will not depart from their ways.

Many of you will not be able to receive this message because some of you still have a judge mentality view (He who is without sin please cast the first stone). I did not write this book for fame or fortune, and through it all, God gets all the glory, I never saw myself as being a writer, and I am amazed at what God is doing in my life at this very moment. Eyes have not seen and ears have not heard what the Lord has in store for me. I am a living witness that God will give you double for your trouble if you just trust. I am glad to know that I have found my Identity in him, and I am proud to say

"I 'M NOT GOING MAD, I'M JUST COMING INTO MYSELF"

AFTER

"LIVING THROUGH DYING PLACES"

Though My Father and
Mother Forsake Me,

The Lord Will Receive Me!

Psalm 27:10

To My Mother Sallie B Walker, who did the best she could in raising an only child, I did not write this book to put neither you or myself on front street, but to Minister to those who may have, or is dealing with the same issues that you and I had to deal with all these years, and through it all, God gets all the glory. I want you to know that I forgive you for all that you have done, even though at the time you were in a dark place and could not see your way through. I want you to know that God kept us and protected us from many dangers seen and unseen, and I thank God for allowing us to be able to get along more than ever before. What we went through did not catch Him by surprise, I love you, and may his grace and mercy continue to bring us closer and closer, for the time is near, and tomorrow is not promised to neither one of us, I know that God has great things in store for the both us, because He is the only one who can give a person double for their trouble, and mend broken hearts, as well as relationships. I pray for you, you pray for me, I love you, I need you to survive, I won't harm you with words from my mouth, because I love you, and I need you to survive, it is his will that every need shall be supplied, you are important to me, and I need you to survive.

With Love: From your one and only son,

Author J'Korey Mills

Chapter One

It was the beginning of summer; I was only six years old when I and my Mother boarded Delta Airlines at Boston's Logan International Air port. I could not understand at the time why we were leaving Boston, but I guess it was for a good cause. When we boarded this huge Air Craft headed to Forrest Park GA. I was given a set of wings by the flight attendant. All I can remember was the fact that my Mother had packed all of my clothes in this big iron steel suit case that was left behind from my Grand Mother (Mary Walker), who died when I was about three years old. It is so funny because I do not recall my Mother packing much of her clothes, but a lot of mine were packed as if I was going to be gone for a long time.

When we arrived at the Williams B Hartsfield Air Port, we were greeted by my cousin Larry who picked us up and drove us to his house and the next day he took us to my Aunts house. Two weeks had gone by and my Mother had to leave to go back to Boston for what I do not know, all she said to me was that she would be back. I did not know who any of these people were, and this was my first time ever meeting them and the only thing I knew bout them was the fact that they were my relatives.

When my Mother left, my Aunt sent me to stay with my cousin Pearl which is her daughter, who had a son by the name of Demetrius (rest in peace). Who lived in what looked like the projects, and cousin Pearl has corrected me to date that they were not projects. While being at her house I began to feel lonely and miserable, I did not want to do anything but stay in the house. Her son would get mad because I did not want to go out and play ball, and neither did I want to do anything else with him. If Pearl had a daughter who liked to play with Barbie Dolls I don't think that I would have been so bored (Laugh out Loud), I enjoyed playing with Barbie dolls, especially with my second generation of cousins who had every Black Barbie doll.

At times I did break through my spirit and went outside, but only for a brief moment, and then I was back in the house in a matter of minutes.

I could not wait until the summer was over; I sat by the door and windows awaiting my Mothers return. Cousin Pearl did not know a thing about cooking, I can remember one Sunday she had cooked some pig's feet and pig ears and I looked at her and told her, that I was not going to eat what she had cooked. I did not know what the hell she was trying to feed me but it was, and looked a hot blessed defied mess, didn't she know I was from the city. I was use to eating fried chicken, pork chops, mashed potatoes and spaghetti and all that good stuff that my Mother use to feed me.

As the summer went on I was introduced to another cousin of mine who is the sister of Pearl, and I left Pearls house to only go and spend the duration of the summer there, with her and her family. When I got there I mainly hung out with the Daughter whose name is Toni, who is only a few years older than me. I enjoyed being at Undine's house, it was like paradise, she was the only one besides Larry that had a clean, decent, smelling and good looking home.

Undine cooked very well, and I can still taste her cabbage in mouth till this very day and she had all the ice cream a child could ever want too eat.

Toni and got along very well, we would either go down the street to play in the school yard and ride bikes or in the back yard. Until one day I got mad at her and called her Ho. Toni went inside and told her Mother what I had said and immediately Undine tore my Ass up with the belt. Toni could not understand why I was getting a whopping; she could not fathom the fact that they were chastising me for something that she though was a garden tool; she really did not know what the real meaning of the word Ho meant. Toni was one of those kids who grew up in a suburban and strict environment were she spent most of her time on lock down by her parents. She was one of those kids who was clueless to the outside world and Still to this very day we laugh and joke about it, which is a good thing, I Love you T.

Summer was about to come to an end and it was time for me to go back to my Aunt's house where I was staying to attend school. I dreaded the fact that I had to go back there, because I had to share a room with my two male cousins. I had to sleep on the top bunk, because Distasteful slept on the bottom bunk, and Stinky slept on the other side of the room in a twin bed. I could not tolerate the fact that I had to stay in the room with them, because the room smelled like a dirty, sweaty, funk-defied gymnasium. I mean it was horrible, and when the two of them ever broke gas, it smelled like open ass on rocks, better yet street booty.

Trying to escape and go into another room did not help much because then you had to deal with the smell of Aunties atomic mouth balls, I swear she could have put Benadryl out of business, no lie (Can The Church Say Yes!!!). What really put the icing on the cake, was the fact that she had roaches, I mean I have never seen so many roaches since I left Boston, and you would have though my Aunt was raising roaches instead of teenagers, that's how bad it was. They would fall from the ceiling, crawling in and around the bath tub, and in the cabinets, and on the couch, and they would even sometimes sleep with you in the bed. She had so many roaches; she could have had a fund raiser, to rebuild Shadrach, her Shack, Meshach, and a few Negro's.

The outside of the house was not all that great; all I wanted to do was, too stay with Larry, or at Undine's, where I knew It was safe and clean, because Pearl had roaches as well.

When I finally got back to my Aunt's house she told me that she had a surprise for me, and I asked her what was the surprise. She handed me three big boxes that my Mother had shipped from Boston, and when I opened them there was nothing but a whole bunch of brand new clothes for me to wear to school. At that moment I began to cry, wondering if she was ever coming back. I did talk with her periodically on the phone, but that didn't help because she never said when she was coming back to get me, and at that moment I felt like I was being abandoned.

There was two weeks left before school had started and I spent most of my time outside playing in Rev. Binn's (Rest in Peace) camper or making mud pies. My aunt lived on a long street that had a dead end to it, and at times there was nothing much for me to do, because I hardly saw any kids playing in and around the neighborhood. I was scared to leave my Aunt's yard because there was this strange man who lived directly across the street from her, and every time I went outside, he would ask me if I wanted some chocolate milk, and if you would have asked me? I think he needed one of those crazy checks (SSI). I asked my Aunt who and what he was, and she told me, and when she told me that he did not mean any harm, and that I did not have to worry about anything, I then felt comfortable enough to leave the yard. Although deep down inside I knew something else was wrong with him, because he was just to flamboyant and sashayed better than RuPaul, oh yes he did the cat walk, up and down his driveway, and that is as far as I ever seen him go, and never once did I see this man leave his yard to go anywhere else.

Here I go being mischievous, and before I knew it I found myself at the dead end part of her street at the Finch's house, that is where I had found some kids to play with. The Finch's had a yard almost the size of a foot ball field and in their yard they had some trucks, the ones you would dig up the ground to do gardening with, and me and the other kids decided to take it upon ourselves and play in one of the tractors, and to only find out that the keys were left inside the ignition. We started it, and before you knew it, we were rolling backwards, scared as hell, not knowing how to stop the damn thing. I thank God for those two twins called Grace and Mercy because that's what brought us through. To this very day Auntie does not know what I was getting myself into and there are some things that children keep in secret and only God knows.

August 1981 School was now in session and I could not grasp the fact that I had to go back to school in the month of August. When back home we did not start school until September, I really did not know much about being in another state, so I had no choice but to go with the flow of things. Don't think for one minute that I was an Angel, because I wasn't, I had a mouth on me, and I could swear and say words that would blow your mind. The school that I attended was the Ash Street Elementary school in Forrest Park Georgia, and my teachers name was Mrs. Queen. I can remember walking through the front entrance, and as you went half way down the corridor; it turned into three different directions, and to the left was the corridor which lead you to my class room.

I don't remember much about what went on in the class room, but I do remember that I use too sit in the second row in the front, and when class began the teacher would take the chalk holder, to make lines on the chalkboard, and then she would write out the assignments on each line for different times of the day.

The one thing that I always looked forward too, was snack time, I would always get the vanilla ice cream bar that was covered in chocolate. So every night before I went to bed I made sure my Aunt or Rev. Binn (Rest in Peace) would give me fifty cents for snack time. I recall a time when I did not get money for snack and I ended up going to school mad as hell at the world, and when it came time for snack I tried to pretend like I had money, knowing dam well I did not have anything at all. I ended up getting caught, and began to act out in an outrage to the point I had to be escorted to principal's office.

I was suspended for three days and when I returned to school I received more punishment, "Well Dam". On the day that I returned to school, the principal came to the class room to get me, and by this time I'm trying to figure out what the hell did I do now. Mind you, I just got back to school, when we arrived at his office, he had a talk with me about why I was suspended, and Before I knew it, this tall Caucasian man went into his desk and pulled out this huge wooden paddle, and told me to put the palms of my two hands out, and before I could blink or utter a word, this man had wacked the shit out of my hands several times. I could not do anything but holler "Mama" hoping that she could hear me all the way in Massachusetts.

After that episode I was about through with being in Forrest Park Georgia, all I wanted to do was to go back home to Boston. I wanted to know who gave those people permission to put their hands on me, because this kind of shit did not go on in Massachusetts, a 51A should have been filed, but I guess they have a way of doing things differently in the dirty south. I did not have any drama until my Mother up rooted me and brought me down here. I was even tired of Auntie beating me with a switch, that she use to send me outside to pick off the tree, and I had better not dare come back with something small and skimpy, because it only made matters worst, because she on the other hand would go and get a fucking branch, and I believe if she was strong enough, she probably would have tried too pull up the tree by its roots. The only thing that I enjoyed was waking up on Sunday Mornings, smelling Auntie's homemade biscuits and that thick maple flavored bacon cooking. The aroma would wake you right up out of bed; even the roaches got up, because they knew their master had cooked, and it was time for them to eat as well. She would also make fried green tomatoes, okra and egg plant; "Ok" I swear these people were trying to kill me; because that too was nasty.

After breakfast Auntie and I would get ready for Church, which was only a few blocks from her house. I don't know what they call a few blocks, because it seemed like forever and a day to walk down those long country roads.

I even had to walk to school the same way. Auntie did not mind it at all; and in fact she still walks to and from church this very day, and all I have to say is God bless you Auntie, to be eighty something, and still able to get up and go, is a blessing from God. We walked Sunday after Sunday and during the week as well to attend choir rehearsals and Bible study.

I can remember singing in the choir with my Aunt and our robes were beige and brown. We traveled everywhere to sing, either with the pastor or just the choir itself for outside engagements. When we had to go places to sing, the two of us either road the church van or car pooled with one of the members who lived on the same street as Auntie. I use to play at this ladies house whenever her Grand Daughter would come over, and sometimes if I was bored and didn't have anything else to do. I would walk down the street and sit and talk with her, and one thing I appreciate was the fact that she never turned me away; in fact she would sit and listen to me talk.

Pleasant Grove was and still is the name of the church my Aunt attends; sometimes we would be there all day long from dusk to dawn, I don't think these people knew what a bed looked like, I sometimes thought my Aunt forgot that I had school the next day. One thing I can say is that no one was without food when it came time to serving dinner in the lower fellowship hall in between services; there was plenty of it to go around even after the evening service. When I look at the churches today, it behooves me to see folk selling food in the church in order to either buy new robes for the choir or for the building fund. I believe the scripture says "I have never seen the righteous begging for bread, neither forsaken". Just think about it, did Jesus charge people for a fish sandwich, when he took two pieces of fish and five loaves of bread to feed a multitude? No! He did not have a seafood restaurant and a menu that stated; fish sandwiches five dollars.

Many of us are using the gifts that God has given us to satisfy our own needs, and is God Pleased? No one should have to pay for food at anytime in the house of the Lord. What makes matters even worst is that I see churches giving outside banquets and charging folk an arm and a leg just to attend these non biblical functions, selling of food in the church has to stop, God is not pleased. If the choir need new robes, wash cars or ask for donations, and if the church is out growing in numbers, then I advise you to go and unite without another church, because that it one of the main issues we have today. We have too many Minister's who claim to be called to teach and preach, and I find that many of them are just using God as a quick and easy way to be employed (Be careful of the faucets that call themselves the source). I'm so glad that I do not have to sit up in a pulpit to proclaim the word God and to receive a check, because the God I serve is cashing checks everyday. I believe God said we are supposed to be one body in Christ, and if you take all the local churches in and around the communities and combine those all into one, then you will have a mega church. The problems is that the leaders can not come together as one because you have some who are stuck and stubborn in their own way and want to run things their way, again I say is this of God? It was fall when I came home from school to only open the door to see my Mother standing there in the kitchen at my Aunts house. When I saw her I grabbed and held onto her for dear life. I was making sure that she was not going to leave me here again with these crazy people. I asked her was she leaving again and she told me no, and that she was here to stay, and that she had left Boston to come and start a new life for the both of us. My Mother eventually got a job working at the electric company on Jimmy Carter Blvd. Apparently My Mother and Aunties Husband Rev. Binn (rest in peace) had made some sort of agreement for her to use his van to go to and from work, until she was able to get on her feet and buy her own car.

Until one day he had asked my Mother for some Money for using the van and she told him that was not the agreement that they had made as far as her getting to and from work. He then took the van away from my Mother leaving her stuck and stranded to get to work, because where she worked there was no bus service and he knew that. She then had to immediately quit her job and go on welfare to support me and her. By this time my Mother had found an apartment; but she could not take it because she was no longer employed and could not afford it.

Eventually we ended up leaving Auntie's house because of an argument that took place between her and Rev. Binn. "Ok" what the hell, back at Pearls house again, but this time I was ok with being there because my Mother was with me. My Mother and Pearl were like two peas in a pod; they both enjoyed partying and liked to have fun. What is so unique about the two of them, is that My Mother is Pearls Aunt and the both of them are around the same age, but pearl is the oldest, "A mess". Pearl would party so hard she would come home drunk slaying in the spirit, and I remember one particular night when pearl came home and me and her son was upstairs supposedly sleeping, and All I could hear were people knocking on her door, and could not understand why these people were coming by her house at 2am in the morning. So I got up and waited for her to go down stairs to open the door, and by that time I was sitting at the top step trying to see what was going on. I could hear pearl telling them to keep quiet because me and her son was sleep, and the fact that it was late, but little did she know that I wasn't, because the eyes of the Lord are in Everything, He does not sleep or slumber. When they came in she immediately directed them to go in the Living room, which was through the kitchen. Once they were out of my sight I went down the stairs and kneeled down at the entrance of the kitchen door too see what was going on. Pearl had a bar that was fleshed to the wall in the Living Room, and from where I was I could see exactly what was going on. I would see her take the bottles of liquor and pour it into the container that they had brought with them, and upon them leaving they would give her money, and now I know to this day, what was really going on, she was the after hour lady.

It was winter of 1982 I was seven years old when a neighbor of Pearls drove me and my Mother to the bus station. It was daylight when we left, Pearl had no idea that me and my Mother had gone, my Mother told her neighbor not to tell Pearl that we had left. Apparently my Mother and Pearl got into one big argument, my Mother was fussing and feuding with her because all Pearl wanted to do was lay up in the bed with all kinds of different men, and if this wasn't the pot calling the kettle black. Pear told my Mother that I was gay and my Mother got upset with her and did not like the fact that she had insulted me. Cousin Pearl was right! I found myself at such a young age starring and looking at boys, there was a time while I was outside playing at Pearls house and me and this other kid was experimenting with one another kissing, and we was caught by the boys Mother who ran next door to tell Pearl to tell her to tell me to stop kissing her son, and Pearl told her to tell her son too stop kissing her cousin.

Chapter Two

When we arrived at Grey Hound Bus station the very next day, My Auntie was there to pick us up in her powdered blue Cadillac. She brought us back to her house where she allowed us to stay. I was happy to finally be back in Massachusetts, and out of the dirty south, there is an old slavery song they use too sing "slavery days are done" and sure enough they were, because I was no longer enslaved to those folk. Before we left Boston I only could remember the good times we had, when I had turned four years old my day care center gave me a birthday party, and at the time I was going too Grove Hall Day Care Center, and my Mother had provided my cake and I remember that cake like it was yesterday. On the cake it showed the scenery of an Indian tribe, and the forts that they lived in, the way it was set up as if they were going to battle.

Eventually I had to stop going to Grove hall day Care because my Mother could not find anyone too pick me up and look after me until she got off from work. I ended up going to stay at this women's house that lived on the other side of the projects while my Mother worked her 9-5. Till one day my Mother had left work to only come home and find out that I did not make it to that women's house that morning. My Mother drove like a bat out of hell, from Waltham to Roxbury in a matter of minutes. She worked for nuclear companies called Raytheon where they build missiles and other electronics as well, and I remember my mother bringing home a clock that she had build while she was working there.

When she arrived at 20 Annunciation Road she saw me sitting on the stairs, I had been wandering around the projects all day long, with out any supervision from any adult. She asked me why I did not go to the baby sitters house, and I told her that I did not want to go there anymore because I was tired of being picked on and teased by this woman's children. I mean her kids use too tease me like there was no tomorrow, and what made matters even worst, was the fact that her house smelled, and looked nasty, and she had roaches galore. I was too afraid to sit or touch or eat anything out of this women's house. I could not wait until my Mother came to pick me up and feed me, somebody should have called the health department, because her house was out of order, better yet, there should have been a sign on her front door that said condemned. In the meanwhile my mother had made some phone calls trying to find me another care taker while she worked and it just so happened that we had a cousin who operated her own Day Care Facility out of her own home, as well as after school care. Out of respect I call her Auntie Dottie, and that is where I ended it up going.

It was a good thing because she was family, and my Mother did not have to worry about me, because I was safe, safe in the arms of someone who loved children and working with them. I loved being there, and she taught me how to write the alphabet, and still I can remember that short thick lined white paper. She would take that paper, and draw the letter that she wanted me to copy a million times, not only did she teach me how to write, but also how to read and color, and cut paper with a pair of scissors. She also had two children of her own Kenyon & Kyran who she also managed to take care of in the midst of taking care of other people's kids. Kenyon and I were born in the same year, but only four months apart, I spent a lot of my time at her house during and after the hours of Day Care, and she would sometimes say to my Mother don't forget Korey. If need be she would have left me there in a heart beat, and it would not have bothered me any because of the fact I was always welcomed to stay. Every time she came to get me, and before we would leave she would sometimes sit down and talk with Auntie Dottie, and I remember going up to her to show her what I had done in school that day, and all I could here her say, "get out of here, grown folks are talking, and I will deal with you later". I thank God for Auntie Dottie because she put her in her place, by telling her that you should not do that to your child, that child has not seen you all day, and the least you could do is show him some love and show interest in what he does.

Auntie D took the time to prepare me for first grade; my Mother had made some sort of arrangements with my Auntie Sadie who lived in Mattapan, to use her address for me to attend the Mattahunt School, which was in walking distance to Auntie Dottie's house. That meant that my Mother did not have to worry about working over time if she needed too. I remember walking home to Auntie D house, and I was bombarded and attacked by two dogs, and I remember when I jumped on somebody's car and screamed "help, help" and before I knew it somebody came running out of their house to rescue me. They were nice enough to walk me half way to her house, and when I ever arrived at Auntie Dottie's she asked me what had happened, and I told her, meanwhile I'm looking for sympathy from her, and all she could ever say was, "Korey stop crying it's going to be alright". Who wanted to hear that shit, did this woman not realize that I was in pain, and the fact that I was just bitten by two vicious dogs. So eventually I stopped crying, and she cleaned up the womb, and I thank God that I did not have to go to the hospital that day because the skin was not broken.

Her husband uncle Johnny (rest in peace) would come home from work and all the kids would run up to him and grab onto his legs as soon as he would walk through the front door, because they were so long, and he was a tall man.

He was a mastermind outside of what he did at his day time job; he had projects that he did in and outside of the house, you name it he did it. He even went to the extreme of rebuilding his Volks Wagon buggy, and he built a tree house in the backyard for Kenyon and Kyran, and what fascinated me the most is when he ripped apart the attic and turned it into another bed room which was for Kenyon, and how the entrance connected to the kitchen and the stair case leading up to the room went in a semi circle. He also made a book case going all the way up the stairs on the wall, and there was a full bathroom and sky lighting windows that ascended outwards. I tell you the truth it was amazing to see him do what he did, my cousin did not have to want for anything, Kenyon had a room that most kids who were less unfortunate would love to have.

There was a time when my school had a candy fund raising project, and I remember all this candy being dropped off at Auntie Dottie's for my Mother to pick up and take to work to sell. She could not wait until my Mother came to pick up the candy because her living room was over filled with boxes, and it was taking away from her décor. Thank you Jesus, because I won that year thanks to my Mother who got her hustle on, and the Raytheon crew who purchased all of the candy. Auntie Dottie is a beautiful caring and loving person, I remember when she took me and the boys to see Marvin Haggler, who was a professional boxer; it was an exciting experience for me, too meet a famous boxer in person, and having the honor to take a photo with him as well. During day care hours Auntie Dottie always had to remind Kenyon & Kyran that their friends could not come into the house until all the Day Care kids were gone, all because if she was ever audited she would have received a fine because she was over her capacity. As soon as Day Care cleared, then came the neighborhood kids, and now it was time for her to show them some love and affection, and she did just that. I don't think this woman has ever received a break from being around children, in fact she loved what she did and still to this very day, she is still working with children, because she is a Grandmother now.

One evening my Mother woke me up to go some where with her, and I was half asleep when she woke me up; and the only thing that I had on was my pajamas. She grabbed her keys and of course her pocket book and headed out the door. When we got to the car she told me to get in the back seat, and I could not understand why all of a sudden I had to sit in the back when normally I sat in the front, riding shot gun. She had a brand new Dodge Diplomat Medallion, with two doors, and with red vinyl interior inside. When we left 20 Annunciation Rd. Roxbury Ma, and drove up Parker Street, which was a street over from our street. We were struck instantly by another vehicle on the rear passenger side. Causing my Mothers car to spin in a complete circle, Thank You Jesus for the breaks, because if was not for those breaks that allowed my Mother to stop, we would have ended up hitting the brick wall, where we could have died instantly. She then backed the car up so fast, and turned around and went after the car that hit us on three wheels, because the front right tire broke, and all you can hear was spectators screaming and yelling, egging my Mother on to go after the other car. They even told her what direction the other car was headed, you would have though you were watching the hit drama TV series Cagney & Lacey, I guess she was Cagney and I was Lacey because Cagney did all the driving.

We eventually caught up with the other vehicle at the corner of Parker and Huntington Ave, a few blocks away from the scene of the accident, by the time we arrived there; the other vehicle was stopped by the Police. My Mother pulled over and got out of the car, I do not know what she told them because I was sitting in the back seat, and I just so happen to turn around and look out the back window to see what was going on. A few seconds later I saw the police putting the other women into hand cuffs, and you could tell she was drunk because her hair was a hot mess, and she could not even stand up straight. After all that was said and done, me and my Mother was taken to a local hospital were she suffered from neck injuries, and little me was alright because God laid his hands on us that night. Come to find out that we were headed to go and pick up my Aunt to take her to the Dog Track (Auntie God Blocked It, wasn't meant for you to gamble that night).

Living in the projects was a sight for sore eyes, people did any and everything, and every time you turned around there was drama. One evening I was sitting in the kitchen eating my dinner, and the kitchen windows were open, because my Mother had just finished frying chicken. While I was sitting there my spirit lead me to go and look out the window, and when I ever went to look out the window I saw this big heavy set woman walking, and carrying a rock in one hand and a beer bottle in another, when I saw that she was heading for my Mothers car I ran into her room and told her that this women was at her car again, my mother immediately ran outside, and before she could get there she had already busted the window. From that point on my Mother had to park her car on the side walk up underneath her window, eventually my mother took her to court and from that point on she did not have any more problems out of this women. The woman who was targeting my Mothers car was the Aunt of a man that one of my female cousins was dating, goes to show you that your own family will get you caught up in their mess, without you having any knowledge of it until the damage is already done.

Chapter Three

One evening; Auntie and my Mother had a big argument, and we ended up having to leave her house in a cab, and ended up going to the sojourner house which was a shelter for families in need, and from there my Mother met with a Social Worker who gave us emergency shelter to stay at a hotel that was located Downtown Boston. We stayed at the hotel for a few weeks; meanwhile my Mother was in the midst of making other arrangements to find some where else for us to go. We finally ended up leaving the hotel to only go and stay with my Auntie Minnie who lived on Cheney St in Roxbury on the first floor, of the house where she and my God Mother, lived in. Before they had moved too Cheney St. I recall them living on Devon St. in an apartment building, where I spent a lot of time there as well.

I was very young, but yet I remember that apartment like it was yesterday, when you entered the apartment my God Mother's bed room was right there as soon as you walked in, and on the left side of her bed room was the living room, and too the left of the living room was another bed room that faced the front of Devon St. As you continued to walk down the hall, the bathroom was too the right and from there you entered into the kitchen, and off the kitchen was another bed room, she had four girls, and each one of them had to share a room with one another.

My Auntie who is my God Mothers, Mother also lived in the projects on Prentiss St., which was only a couple of blocks from Annunciation Rd, where my Mother and I use too live. when my God Mother bought the three family house on Cheney St., it was a blessing for them to have that house, because it gave them more living space. Auntie Minnie lived on the first floor with two of the Divas, and my God Mother on the second floor with the other two Divas. They also had a dog named Akia who spent most of his time in the back hallway, and a black cat named Sheek who was privileged to be in the house.

I hated the fact that the dog stayed in the back hall way, because it was hard for me to go up and down the backstairs by myself, without having any fear that I was going to be attacked by the dog. The Divas use too yell at me, because I would make one of them hold the dog while I went up and down the stairs, and I guess they were getting sick of the fact that I was scared of the dog. One of the Divas did not make the situation any better, she would always tried too torment me with the dog, by trying to have him to bite me, she also treated me mean by calling all kinds of horrible names, every other day I was a sissy or a fagot and often times she would get caught calling me these names by my Godmother, and she would get yelled at.

Her getting yelled at did not stop her at all, she continued on, and whenever her Mother was not around she would use undertone statements as if I could not hear her. I Love her to this day, and I'm glad to say that we can look back and laugh about it, but at the time it was not humorous to me because I was already having identity issues. She did have some good in her back then, but I often question what her intentions were to this day, she gave me work to do out of one of her school books, when I had to stay home with her throughout the day while everyone else was either at school or at work. I wonder if she was doing it out of love, or was it because her Daytime Soaps were on and that was a quick and easy way to get me out of her hair for a few hours.

I loved my God Mother very much, because she out of a few took up time with me. I would always look forward to the weekends; she would pack a cooler that was full of Pepsi and Mountain Dew. She would also fry chicken and beef hot sausages, which you had to eat with four pieces of bread because they were so hot, and she would pack those in the cooler along with everything else. She would take me and her youngest daughter to her soft ball games that were played at one of the local parks in Boston Ma. We drove in style; she had a canary yellow Cadillac Broham, which also had a brown rag top roof, which was fully loaded with an eight track cassette player, with brown leather interior inside.

My cousin would always sit in the front riding shot gun, which didn't bother me any, because sitting in the back was like riding in a limo, my God Mother had one of the top of the line Caddy's. Her soft ball team called themselves the Jetetts who played against other teams, the Jetetts not only played soft ball they gambled too, taking turns hosting cards games at one another's house. I know because I was dragged by my Mother to a lot of those late night card games, and no my Mother did not play soft ball, but yet she went to all the card games they had, and sometimes I did not mind going because there were other kids there to play with.

I must say that I enjoyed Christmas at My God Mothers house; she would buy trees that were as big as a Giraffe, and fat like a Hippopotamus. Where did she ever find trees that size, and how, and who helped her bring them in the house. I do not know who helped her, but all I can say is that after it was all decorated it looked absolutely beautiful. It was one year we had to unload the tree on Christmas Eve, because there were too many gifts underneath it, and they were over flowing into the traffic area of the house. Eventually we ended up moving out and into our own apartment, and my mother had landed a job working for Bank of Boston, which was located on Morrissey Blvd, Dorchester Ma. At this time she had retrieved all of our belongings out of the basement of her Brother in Laws house. That's where she had everything stored, when she finally left Boston to come to Georgia, and she found out that somebody was stealing some of her stuff, because some things of hers was missing, and that her Brother In Law was encouraging her to come and get our belongings out, for the simple fact that he knew what was going on with some of our stuff, my cousin, his son, was going through our stuff and selling it to people in the streets.

When we finally moved into 17 Winter St, She had bought me a new bunk bed, and the only thing that I did not like about it was the fact that you could not separate the beds, but again, I was grateful, because I had a room again and a bed to sleep in. My Mother did not have any problem with telling me to keep my room clean, because I did it anyways, as well as the rest of the house. Not to long after we moved in, my privacy was turned up side down, because she allowed my Uncle a place to stay, who was a truck driver for a meat packaging company. What made matters even worst was the fact that he had to sleep in my room, and I had to give up the bottom bunk and sleep up on the top. Whenever he came home to our house, he would head straight for my room and take off his nasty smelling funk-defied boots, as well as his clothes, which reeked of raw meat. I was now too uncomfortable of being in my own room and wanted him the hell out. I could not take it any more, I did what any child would do, and I kept quiet and did not tell my Mother how I felt. Back then; it didn't matter how children felt, you just had to deal with what ever was thrown your way, and your feelings did not matter at all. I spent most of my time in the living room until he got his ass the hell out, and "Oh Happy the Day" when he finally moved out, because I had to go in my room like I was the swat team from CSI, "Oh yes", it was a crime scene that had to be investigated. I mean I had to disinfect and wash down, and clean up the funk he had left. What mad it even worst, is the fact that he ate in my room, and would leave dirty dishes all over the place, and my Mother did not say one word, but let me do some shit like that, I would get the shit kicked out of me. Although I am a neat freak, it just bothered me that he was filthy; it was bad enough that we already had roaches, but not like the ones at my Aunts house in Georgia.

At times it was fun living on Winter Street, we all use too play in the hall way when it began to get dark outside. My Mother had some friends of her own that lived in the building as well, and I remember one particular night she had went out with the people down stairs, and I had to be baby sat by the son, who had a older cousin that was practically there all the time, and as a young man, I found myself starring at him and thinking impure thoughts, yes he was very attractive and good looking with a medium built body with brown hazel eyes. What made him more attractive was the fact that he had a scar on the left side of his face, having these feelings, and no one to talk to about them was a hard thing to deal with, I began to question myself and my identity, trying to figure out what was going on with me. I guess you can say that, **I'm not going Mad; I'm just beginning to come Into Myself.**

My Mother gave herself a nice house warming party, even though I had to stay in my room with no one to play with, and the next day I did all the cleaning and looked at the things she had received for the house, and I must say she received a lot of nice things. The surprised birthday party she gave me was very nice and I thank her and my cousin who helped her put it all together. Christmas that year was a blast, because by that time my Mother and my Aunt had settled their differences, because we ended up over her house that year for Christmas dinner.

Chapter Four

1983 I was placed in a residential school, I was eight going on nine years old, and I could not fathom the fact of why I was being taken out of my home; it was a tough assignment trying to gather all of what was happening to me. As time went on I began to come to some sort of understanding of why I was being placed in residential, as I can remember I had some issues with being in the public school system, I had a hard time with learning the assignments in the class room, and it was also hard for me to keep up with the other peers. Whenever I came home there was no one there to help me with my home work, and when my Mother came home she could not help me as much. She was just as clueless as I was, and she use too make me more frustrated, because she though I did not want to do the work, and yelled and screamed at me because I was seeking help. When in fact I was really having difficulties, and she would always assume that I was doing things deliberately, just to get on her nerves and she would constantly throw up in my face, and tell me how much I reminded her of my father, like that was supposed to make me feel any better. As time went on my behavior in school began to get out of hand, and I was eventually suspended for assaulting the teacher, because I felt that I was not getting enough help, and was frustrated with the school work. When it was time for me to return to school, there was a big meeting that took place, they suggested that I needed outside therapy, and from that point on I went to see a therapist after school, and I remember one day when the Therapist came to the house, and because I would not let her in the house, she called my Mother who was at work, and told her that I would not open the door, and I recall my Mother telling that lady that I was not going to let her in, because of the fact that I thought they were coming to take me out of my home. Evidently outside therapy was not enough for me, and my behavior had worsened since my last episode, and another meeting was called and at this meeting they decided that public school was not the place for me, and that I needed much more help than what they could offer. So from that point on they had expelled me from school, and before I knew anything, they had filed a 51a on my Mother who then had to fight the system in family probate court Downtown Boston, She lost her case, and at that moment I felt her pain, because I was hurt as well to know that I was going too live in a residential facility, and not be at home with my Mother.

Here I am at The Home for Little Wanderers on South Huntington Ave, Jamaica Plain Ma, where I spent four years of my life, "Ok, if this wasn't like Prison, somebody please tells me what was really going on". I lived two years as a residential student, and the other two years as a day student, it was scary to know that I would not be living at home with my Mother, and going into this place was mind boggling, and does anyone have a clue about how I felt mentally? I had difficulties getting along with other peers, and adjusting to a new atmosphere. I had to share a room with others, and eventually that did not work out too well, because I was either arguing, or fighting with someone, and what made matters worst is that half of them were not as clean as I was. After a while I was transferred into a single room (Thank You Jesus), and I only went home on the weekends and during the holidays, this was a twelve month program and the doors never closed.

My Mother did not help by calling me, because by the time I got off the phone I was a mess, a complete mess, crying, distraught, and not knowing what the hell was going on, and why was all of this happening, and where the hell was my Father at. I had to face all of this alone, and deal with my peers calling me names, horrible names at that; I was constantly reminded that I was gay, and a fagot, sissy, homo. Well like they said what's done in the dark will come to the light, and sure enough it did, after a while I started finding out that there were some individuals who was doing the name calling, having identity crisis themselves. For the simple fact, that I had an interest in this one kid, whose room was directly across from mine, and periodically we would meet up in the bathroom to fool around. R.H was very attractive, and he was at least two years older than me, or more, because he was in the mainstreaming class, and when he left to go on to another residential program I was upset. Often times when it was time for me to make my phone call to call home, I use to wait for staff to leave the office, and upon them leaving I would get the phone list, that hung right above the phone that had all the names and numbers of all the other residential facilities, that was affiliated with The New England Home, and I would call the program that he was at. Eventually he faded away from my mind, and I was now being distracted by another Resident, who also left the program and continued residential treatment at the same program as R.H.

KCC is the actual name for the program that I was in, and New England Home is the name of the company that manages different alternative programs in and out of the Massachusetts area. KCC, stands for Knight Children's Center, and they also operated a day program for children who lived at home, and is not capable to attend the Public School system for behavioral, or learning disabilities. The residents were divided into groups of threes; there were the Jaguars, Panthers & Cobras, when I first started being a resident I was first a Jaguar, and then I eventually was transferred to the Panthers where I met R.H. The class rooms were broken up as well into fours; there was the Pumpkins' Hobbits, Super Stars & Rangers. The Pumpkin's was the beginning class for children who were under the age of six, and when I started class, I started as a Hobbit, and R.H was a Ranger, which was the mainstreaming class for everyone. I Got there eventually, thank you Jesus!, R.H was special to me, because he was the first male that I have ever gotten intimate with at such a young age, I don't even recall what it felt like, and what I was thinking at the moment, but when I look back, I don't regret what happened, because I saw it for what it was, I realize that

"I WAS NOT GOING MAD; I WAS JUST COMING INTO MYSELF".

I would always end up in some kind of trouble, either it would be in the time out room, or in a Physical hands on restraint. I had, and still have a mouth, and I know how to use it very well, and even to this moment in my life, Amen! I was, and I am temperamental, but only when provoked, and if you got in my way, you were in deep trouble, because I would black out and just start throwing all kinds of shit, chairs, pens books, and pencils. Whatever I could get my hands on, was heading for you and I did not give any warning signals, "No" there were no traffic lights to tell you too slow down and proceed with caution, but now I give people warnings to back off, and by the third one, you better run like hell, because I will tell you about yourself in so many words, and say things that will make your head spin, and it's a shame that sometimes I have to act like I'm crazy, in order for people to get the message, to leave me the fuck alone, even to this very day I still have to come out of character. I say this; if I'm not bothering you, back the fuck off and leave me alone, I am Gods mess, and you don't have to deal with me. It is a shame that you have to go the extra mile to make people leave you the hell alone, after you have given them forewarning.

It would almost take six staff members to get me back under control, and I hated being restrained, because some of those staff members were both big and fat, or their mouth stunk like Hog's Head Cheese or better yet Brunswick stew, and sometimes like shit, and I wondered sometimes if they were eating ass, or if their ass was coming out of their mouths.

While I was a residential student, I was able to participate in my church Activities throughout the week. I sincerely thank God for Sister Ann Gerald, who was in charge of the Southern Baptist Junior Choir, and was the director as well. I was baptized at this church, and served as a Junior Usher. I could not wait until Thursday nights came, because after dinner I would go up to my room or sit and wait in the staffs lounge by the window, awaiting for this big white two door Chevy Impala, that had a red rag top roof, with white vinyl interior inside. All you can see was the head of this woman driving this big car that reminded me of the women from the Where's the beef commercial, back in the eighties. I grew attached to her, and all the other kids in the choir were jealous of our relationship, and they felt as though she was giving all her attention to me "Favor Is Not Fair, But Necessary In the sight of God". I hated when rehearsals was over because that meant that I had to go back into captivity, and upon me returning to my unit I would sing out loud to the extremes where I would wake everyone the hell up. Staff always had to tell me to be quiet because the other residents were asleep; I paid them no attention, and I still sung my songs, because I was happy, happy down in my little soul, and nobody got the glory but God.

Sister, Gerald was like my own American Idol, I loved the way she sung, and how she directed the choir, and not only was she the director for the children's choir, she was also the director of the senior choir. The Senior choir always sung on the second, and fourth Sunday of every month, and the junior ushers also ushered on those Sundays as well, When I ushered those particular Sundays, my only concern was ushering the choir into the church, and into the choir stand, and ushering them around the church when it came time for offering, and after that I considered my job being done. That was the only excitement that I got out of being an Usher, besides attending those boring annual candle light services. You could not get me to serve on the floor, I hated being on the door and in the isles. Sister Holly who was our Supervisor and Bernard who was the President would make me mad whenever they made me serve in the isles. I would have a fit when they would let someone else take my place when it came time for processing the choir into the church, and during offering, when the choir had to be lead around the church, and back into the choir stand. I can still hear Sis Gerald and others singing their songs, as lead vocalist with the choir, (Some Glad Morning), and Sis Sandra White, who was the superintendant of the Sunday School Department, singing (Stepped Out On His Promise) By Dorothy Norwood, this song is one of my all time favorites, and Sis Ball, (All Of My Help) and Sis Wilson (Till I Die), and Brother Earl Frost who is still hanging tough as the organist, (Lord Keep Me Day BY Day,) By the Caravans.

Those songs bring back many memories, and I still carry them inside my heart, mind, body and soul to this very day. Music that means something and sounds so good never gets old, neither played out. There are times where I find myself at home directing the walls, imitating Sis. Gerald and the rest of the Choir, you might think I am crazy, but I still carry on, directing my walls to date, and I tell you that my walls is the best choir you will ever find, because the members don't talk back and there is no feuding and fighting, me and my walls have a extravagant good time in the Lord. Again I Say God gets all the glory because he said when one or two are gathered in my name, he is in the midst, which goes to show you that **"I'M NOT GOING MAD; I'M JUST COMING INTO MYSELF"**.

My Aunts and their Girlfriends would get tickled pink watching me ushering, especially when I processed the choir into the church. They would tease me, but in a good way, and often times when I am around them they will constantly remind me, especially as I grew older. I missed a few rehearsals sometimes because of my behavior, but in the midst of it all I still gave God the praise.

When Birthdays came around, everyone was given a party, and everyone on the unit had to participate, and you were allowed to invite two guess from another unit. The only thing that was important to me was the fact of having my Mother there, and what surprised me, is that she brought my favorite cousin Darlene to my party. Everyone was allowed to pick a dinner of their choice, and it was submitted to the kitchen staff to prepare, not only that, you also received a Birthday cake as well, and gifts that came from the toy closet that was presented to you by your Advocate. Parents would also bring gifts, and some even provided their own birthday cakes. That night I chose to have Hot Pastrami and Corn Chowder, which was my favorite, and not knowing that my cousin was coming to visit, I realized that she liked Hot Pastrami too, I learned a lot being at KCC, as I look back, I realize that I was a work in progress, because they were basically teaching me some things I needed to learn which was life skills. In June of 1985 I mainstreamed back home to live with my Mother as a fulltime day student.

Chapter Five

Shortly after returning home from the residential program, we ended up having to move. This time we went to go and stay with a friend of my Mothers who worked at the bank with her. We ended moving because my Mother could no longer afford to pay the rent. I hated being at this women house because there was no life to it, her house was dark and gloomy, and dull looking, and I don't think this women even knew when it was day light, because the sun did not even shine through the windows, and further more she never opened up her shade to let the sun come through. I and my Mother stayed in her extra room that she had, and this women had a son that was in and around the same age as me, and I did not care much for him, and one thing I can say is that she did attend church, because I would some times go with her and her son to their weekly evening services. My Mother ended up storing all of our furniture in my Aunts Garage, and the only thing that she brought with us was my bunk bed, which was a smart idea, because we at least had something to sleep on, and she ended up having too buy new linen for both top and bottom bunk, and of course I slept on the top. At times I spent most of my time in the room and did not socialize with them at all until my Mother got there; it was a tough situation, because when I came home I was use too putting a key through the door.

Not this time around, I had to wait until the son got home from school before I could get in, and I thank God that he was home to let me in. His Mother was strict on him, and he was not allowed to go outside when he came home from school. Before I left school I always made sure that I had extra stuff to do at home, I would ask the teachers for extra work, or I would make photo copies of pictures out of books, so that I had something to color or cut too make little projects, and My Mother made sure I had crayons and note pads, and other things as well to keep busy.

One evening I herd my Mother and the women arguing, they argued so bad to the point where she told us to leave her house. I was kind of glad to be leaving, but my only question was, "where the hell were we going to move too now", and what was going to happen to my bed? My Mother made some sort of arrangements to move the bed and other things we had out. Where did she store it? Is a good question, because I know the bed did not go into my Aunts garage with the rest of our belongings? While we were living with this women me and my Mother would sometimes go out and do things, I remember one Sunday evening she took me to see Karate Kid at the movie theatre, that was playing in fields corner, and not too far from where we was staying, and often times I sit back and continue to watch those child hood movies and it feels good to remember something that was once positive and good.

We ended up going to stay with another girlfriend of hers, that Lived around the Corner on Bowdoin St. this women had two boys of her own, and we were there for only a brief moment, I guess so that my Mother can gather her thoughts and figure out the next plan of action, which was to go and stay with my cousin on Schuyler St. "What the Hell" it was ok until my cousin told my Mother that we had to move because her man did not want us to stay there anymore, it's a shame too see what people would do for a piece of dick, and still to this day all she cares about is a piece of dick, and what she needs to do is learn how to sit with self and get to know self. I never liked her, and never once did I get along with her, and there was a time when we were living on Winter Street, and she was babysitting me, and something transpired between the both of us that made me upset, and triggered me to go after her, and kick her ass. Too this very day she threatens me, by telling other family members, that if she ever saw me at another family function that she was going too treat me like one of the niggas on the streets, in other words she was trying to say that she was going to take her gun that she has in possession, and shoot me. What brought all of this about was the fact that I told her about herself in so many words, and she could not take what I had to say to her, but people don't seem to realize children remember nasty, and mean things, and how they were treated by others, as they grow into adult hood, and like Madea said, don't wait to the person is dead and gone to express how you feel, because by then it is too late.

They forget what they have done, to make another human being feel the way they do towards them, and when the tables turn they can't take what is coming. No! "I am not going mad or better yet what she tells other people, that I am Bipolar, I am just now continuing to come into who I am in Jesus".

Like she told me at one of our family functions, that everyone knows I Love the Lord, and to answer that question, "Yes-I-do", because he said Vengeance is mine, you reap what you sew, and if you reap of good things, then good things shall you reap, if you reap of bad things, bad things shall you reap, people don't realize that the power is in the tongue, and that is why many of you are suffering today and don't know how to pull out of the situation that you are in, we wrestle not against flesh and blood, but evil and wicked spirits, and principalities that are in high places.

She also has said that no one listens to me, when I speak or say things, but I want her to know that I am not talking to her, and that there is more than a hand full of people out there who would love to here something nice, and encouraging, and where ever God sends me I will go, because his grace is sufficient, and it was him that brought me through all this shit, and to tell of this testimony to bless someone else, and to let them know again, you are not alone, and all is not lost, if you only begin too let go, and let God, and seek your true identity in him.

Then you can only begin to imagine how victorious the out come will be, yes you will have to go through some things when you began to walk with God, and No! The roads are not going to be easy, for this race was not giving to the swift or the strong; it was given to those who will endure it until the end, for example: writing this book and reliving what I went through was a taught assignment, but again I say God gets all the glory.

In the midst of your walk, God will do some things that will blow your mind, and there will be tests of your faith, "oh yes", God will test you, but always stand guard for the enemy does come to kill, steal and destroy.

Another reason why we can't grow, we spend too much time blaming and giving the Devil the victory, when in fact it is God trying to speak to you, and you do not listen, if things do not turn out the way you want them too, its because God knows best, God will give you things that you so eager to have but in the right timing, just to show you this battle is not any of ours, and it belongs to him. The real issue is that people like her, have a hard time with facing the fact that we cant run this race without God, and the reason why people keep failing over and over, is because of the fact that they try to do it on their own, but can't come to grips with the fact that we need God in every aspect of our lives, he has a master plan for each and everyone of us, and many of you are scared to surrender and let God take full control because of the fact of not knowing the unknown. God said "your ways are not my ways, and your thoughts are not my thoughts, in other words God is saying that his thoughts are higher than any of ours, and our ways are not His ways, prayer is the key and faith unlocks the door, and faith without works is dead.

What makes matters worst is the fact that her daughter can be a bitch, and an ungrateful one at that, and little do she know I use to drag her little ass to church, and get her dress and sometimes I had to do her hair by putting her hair in two afro puffs, when she was just a baby, that's why I do not fucks with them, because they are some ungrateful motherfuckers.

No matter what you try to do for them or for anyone else they will still have something to complain about, and then get mad because they feel as though you are meddling in their business, when you comment or give constructive advice, well if you don't come to people with your problems, and learn to take them to Jesus, then you wont have to worry about people being in your business (Hallelujah & Amen). Let the truth be told about the night her brother was killed, he was on his way to kill someone, and it backfired, that person ended up killing him in self defense, I tell you the truth, this family has more secrets than Victoria. Now I have come to understanding to why her brother had this floral arrangement that sat on the top of his casket with the initials T.S.P, it was the initials of the gang that he was a member off. Jesus told his disciples on the day when he was arrested, when they begun too draw their swords to fight, he told them to put them away, and he said if any man shall live by the sword, surely shall they die by the sword (Mathew 26:50-52). They continue to say I'm crazy, yes I may be a little crazy, but in fact, I'm crazy for Jesus, and I don't have a problem with speaking my mind, God did not put me here on this earth to kiss ass, nobody's at that. I can understand why her sister stays to her self, and it's very rare that you would see her come to family gatherings. I always hated when my Mother would ask her to babysit me, and from that point on, I and my Mother went into a shelter in Brockton Ma.

Here I am eleven years old taking a bus from Brockton to Jamaica Plain Ma, just to go to school. Periodically I would sometimes go back to my Aunt's house after school, that lived on Cheney St, and meet my Mother, and then the two of us would ride the bat bus back to Brockton. Sometimes I was too early for school, and I would go to my Aunts house in the morning and wait a while until it was time for me to head on to school, this only happened when my Mother had to come into Boston to take care of some Business prior to my normal time of departure. Other than that she was at the shelter waiting for me to return home form school, "yes" I called the shelter home, because it was a place to sleep, and we was not sleeping on no park bench in the Boston Commons, or in a MBTA train station, (Thank You Jesus). One thing I liked about the shelter is that I had my own little private room right next door to my Mothers, and she had a little hot plate that she would cook off of to feed us, and also a cooler that she would fill up with ice to keep our food cold and fresh. I think there was a refrigerator in the room as well, and the only real decent meal I had was either in school, and the time when we went to her friend's house, who use to work with her at Raytheon. This woman lived in Randolph which was a couple towns over from Brockton, and she came to pick us up one Saturday evening from the shelter to go over her house and have Chinese food. It was fun going over there because she had two boys, and one of them I believe was her foster child, and I think that they were in the process of adopting him, but something ended happening, (and as quieted as kept, there is a family member in our family who is adopted, and don't even know it, which is sad, I say this, at least tell that individual the truth, and give them the common courtesy of finding out who they real parents are, and the fact that they was adopted, because what is done in the dark, will eventually come to the light!).

Her other son was her biological son, and I remember when he was just a baby, and when I ever saw his picture on Face Book, I saw nothing but this spitting image of his Mother in him. Her Mother also lived in Randolph on Fredrickson Dr. I remember us having Easter dinner there, and them having an Easter egg hunt for all the kids. I'll never forget it, because it was the first time I had ever eaten Keisha and Patty, "Laugh out Loud" (Quiche & Pate`).

Eventually we moved out the shelter in Brockton and moved into another shelter in Dorchester Ma, called the Swiss Chalet` which is now known as the Ramada Inn, and next door was and I think? Still is a Bowling Alley and Arcade where I spent most of my time playing video games, whenever we or I had extra money. By this time My Mother was back on Welfare and we could not afford much, and I eventually became friends with some of the staff that worked at the front desk, and as time went on they started to ask me some questions about my personal life and why was me and my Mother living there. I did not consider them being nosey, because if you take a good look at what was going on, you would wonder yourself, it's not a normal everyday thing; too see a family living in a hotel. I told them that our house was in a fire, why? Because I was too embarrassed to tell them what was really going on and the fact that I did not know them very well, even though they were nice to me and treated me like a human being. Often times they would ask me to run errands for them, when they were not able to leave the front desk to go dinner or lunch, or even too go get coffee from Dunkin Doughnuts, and they use to buy me little things, and often times they would tell me to keep the change that was leftover.

There was one guy, who worked the front counter, and for some reason or another we became close, this was different because he was a Caucasian male who had to be in his early twenties, and he was very attractive, and the only sad part is that he had a girlfriend (Damn, Damn, Damn, Damn, as Florida Evans would say) This man attended college at UMass Boston, and sometimes when it was not busy, you would see him in the lobby doing his home work. What really caught my attention was the fact that he did not judge me, and he treated me very well. He was like a brother from another Mother, and what surprised me even more is that he was a Christian, and often times he would invite me to go with him to bible study groups. I went, and I must say it was different, but as God says when one or two are gathered in his name, he is in the midst. It did not matter who and what you were, God did not appoint any of us by the color of our skin, and what we did and how we did it, He created us all to be one body in Christ. I was grateful for him because our relationship continued even after we had moved out of the Hotel. This man bought me a gift On my birthday, and in fact we walked across the street to purchase it from what use to be Bradlees, and that meant a lot to me considering the position that me and my Mother was in, and the fact that she could not afford to buy me much, like she use too, but she manage to buy a little something, with what little she had. My Mother liked him, but I know she did not like the fact that he had bought me what I have always wanted since the day they came out, and I remember people trying to kill one another just to buy a Cabbage Patch Doll; I had every intention on getting a Black doll, but what a surprise, there was no more black dolls left. The fact of me wanting one so bad, I ended up getting a Caucasian Doll, whose head was bald, and who had the same name as they guy who was purchased it.

There was one other Caucasian male who was the general manager of the hotel and who is Italian, and he also had a beautiful wife. This man went to the extremes of inviting me over to his house, and often times he would give me free tokens to use at the arcade, and often times he would take me out to eat. This man was more like a Father figure for me, and when I look back and see where God has brought me from, I thank God because those two men were Angels in the midst of all the turmoil. This is why people miss out on their blessings, because they are so quick to judge one another, and a lot of times what you are judging and looking down upon could actually be your blessing, and Guess what you just missed it. I have realized that our blessings come to us in many ways, some small and some big and people missed them because of their ignorance towards others. If you don't believe then I advise you read the story about Peter how he was in the water, and how God sent him three boats, and when each one of them stopped to rescue him, he told them to go ahead, and that he was waiting on God. "Guess what"? God showed up, but Peter did not realize it until God told him that he had already sent him help.

I hated the fact that my school bus and church van had to come and pick me up at the hotel, and I always wondered what people were thinking about me having to be picked up at a hotel, and I did not volunteer any information unless someone wanted to get in my Business, and still I did not disclose the truth. I would tell the kids on the bus who would inquire, that my Mother worked there, and that she was the General Manager. I put my Mother on a pedal stool; all because I was hiding my feelings too avoid the embarrassment of telling them that I lived there, and the fact of me just wanting to shut them up so that they can stay out of my business. The people from church really didn't ask me questions, thank you Jesus because we all know how nosey and trifling they can be.

We continued to cook our food on the hot plate that she brought from the previous hotel and purchased, and we continued to keep our food cold in coolers, and it even got so bad that my Mother started using the tub as a refrigerator by using ice from the vending machine, and we had to keep the hot plate hidden from house keeping, because we were not allowed to have them in the hotel, but what was a person supposed to do when there back is up against the wall. My God Mother was the only one who came to see about us, and I remember the day she came, because she had just bought a new mid size sports car, and got rid of the Cadillac, I was not too happy when I found out, that she traded it in for something that looked like one of my Hot Wheels, I believe she was going through or having mid life crisis, because that car did not fit her at all, and "guess what" she eventually ended up back in a Cadillac.

Finally we moved out of the shelter into a three family house on Alpine St. in Roxbury Ma, after moving, I found out that we had to endure all that pain in order for my Mother to obtain her section 8, which is a certificate for people who can not afford to pay market rent. Thank you Jesus! I enjoyed the fact that we was moving to that particular street because it was in walking distance to my Aunts house and Church, and The Boys and Girls Club of Roxbury. My Mother had rented a truck, and had some of my male cousins and their friends to move our belongings out of my Aunts garage, and once again it felt good to finally have my own room again, and what I liked about it was the fact that it was big and spacious and it gave me more room to do some rearranging. Out of the blue my Bunk Bed was retained, and I don't know where she had stored it, but Thank You Jesus, that it was not lost and that I had a bed to sleep in. Our apartment had the best view, it overlooked Circuit and Washington St. and high above the ground stood the train tracks of the Orange Line that went from Forest Hills station to Oak Grove. There was a twist to riding that particular line, being on that train while it was pulling into Dudley station was a pisser, because the train would enter in a S, C shape form, where it looked like the tail end of the train was not going to make it around the corner, and the fact that the train was above ground made the situation look even worst than it was.

I spent most of my time at the Boys and girls club where I met a lot of good people, and some of them lived in my neighborhood. I never really had any problems at the club, because I was one of those kids who minded his business and stayed to himself, until the night when I was about to leave the club to go home. I witnessed a stabbing outside of the club, it was horrifying to see this kid being stabbed with a knife several times. I would have ran inside to seek help, but back then you were taught to mind your business, and I did not want to be the one they would come after next for being a snitch.

I managed to get along well with some of the kids in my neighborhood, and yes we did have neighborhood bullies who use to pick on me when ever I was walking home, and sometimes if I saw them at afar, I would detour and go into another direction to avoid them, because I knew they were either going to follow me and jump me for no apparent reason, and yes I have gotten the shit kicked out of me on numerous occasions' by neighborhood gangs. It is a shame that you cant even walk down your own street, or anywhere else without being picked on for no apparent reason, I still can't understand why people want to walk around and dehumanize another human being, now I can say "no one can move my mountain" because I have learned that I have nothing too fear, and my biggest fear in life now is God!

I continued going to KCC as a Day Student, and I still continued getting picked up by the yellow short bus. I can say that my Mother had a lot of men in and out of her life, and most of them were pretty descent until the day she met 1st & 2nd Samuel, and believe me there was no comparison to the real Biblical 1st and 2nd Samuel, because this man had two sides of him. My Mother met this man at a girlfriend's house during Thanksgiving one year, and before I knew it, he was moving in, this was a first because my Mother never had any man living with us, they may have spent the night and got their rocks off, but that was about it (Children are not stupid, for the eyes of the Lord are in everything we do).

As time went on he took us to meet his Mother and the rest of the family, he was nice and charming at first, and he had a son by another women, and often times I could not figure out why he did not spend time with his son or at least let me or my Mother meet him. In the midst of all this I felt something about him that was not right, and I did not trust him and I started to become over protective of my Mother. There were times when my Mother would leave for work, and I had to take care of myself and be responsible in getting myself ready for School, and be on time for when the school bus came.

He would walk around the house in his Bath Towel after him taking his shower trying to intimidate me by showing off his masculinity, as if I was supposed to be scared of him, and often times he would walk around half naked deliberately, just so that he can say nasty and mean things to me, because he thought I was looking at him as if I wanted him. But what bothered me is the fact that he had a brother who was Gay, and at this point I knew I had to put on the whole armor of God, because I was about ready too kick his black Jerry Curl wearing ass.

One morning we finally ended up bumping heads and I ended up missing my school bus because of it, and I had to call my Aunt to come from Mattapan to Roxbury to take me to school because I had missed the bus, why? Because he was being rude, ignorant and nasty towards me, and my temper explode to the point where I went the fuck off in fighting this ignorant ass of a man. "Yes" he may have been taller than me and older, but I did not care, and what respect did he deserve, respect is given when earned, did his parents not teach him that, although they were born again Christians, and they have the nerve to give their children names, of characters out of the bible.

I told my Aunt what happened and when I got to school I told my Case Manager and told her that I was not going back home. My case manager then called my Mother and explained to her what happened, and that she wanted to meet with her and me to see what was going on, and to see if the issue could be resolved. I don't know why she called her, because all she cared about was him, because there were times when I would seek her attention and knock on her room door, and he would answer, and ask me what I wanted, as if my Mother was in captivity.

Did she forget that she had a child; it was horrible I had to go through him just to speak to her. Periodically I would catch her in the midst of walking down the hallway to go into the kitchen or the bathroom, and that would be the only time that I would have had the opportunity to say something to her, I could not do anything but keep my feelings to myself, and how is a eleven year old suppose to grasp all of what was going on, with no support from anyone.

The meeting did not go as well because I was afraid to talk, I knew that all she cared about was a man to show her love and affection, and adults sometimes have a tendency of not listening to children until it is too late, (I say this to say, No parent should ever put their feelings before their child's feelings).

My feelings did not matter to her at all, my Mother was selfish when it came to him and other men, she would keep her self locked up in the room as if I did not exists. He was a manipulator, and what got me is that he wore a different mask when ever she was home, but when she was not there, all hell would break loose. So I started spending more time at my aunts house, just to get away from him, and what made matters even worst is the fact that he was also a vegetarian, and he did not like the fact that we ate meat, and tried to change our way of living, "God Blocked

It", and I remember him throwing all of our food out of the freezer onto the floor because there was nothing there for him to eat, and the times he would make me go to Dudley Station to get him a vegetarian sub from Spinale's, which was right next door too one of my favorite places too eat Churches Chicken. Right then, and there my Mother should have put his ass the fuck out, I guess love will make you stupid and blind, because after that episode they ended up getting married, "W-H-A-T-T-H-E-F-U-C-K". I continued on going to school day in and day out, holding in the pain that this man had caused me, not being able to talk to anyone, because all adults seem to think is that children only tell lies. She also told me once before that I needed to stop my shit, because she felt as though I did not want to see her happy with anyone, and that I was trying to ruin her life. Somebody please tell me what parent in there right mind says those kind of things to an Eleven year old.

My Mother ended up calling the wedding off the day before it was supposed to happen, all because he did not have the money to pay for his Tux, and him not being able to up hold his financial portion of the wedding, hours later the wedding was put back into play, and my Mothers girlfriend was nice enough to charge his Tux on her credit card, and he was responsible for paying her back. The wedding and the reception ended being an all in one, because they had to cut out a lot of expenses, including the church, and there was only one wedding rehearsal that I can remember, so everything ended up being at my Aunts house in Mattapan. Food was not an issue because my Mother had already delegated family members and friends of hers too cook certain dishes for the reception, and her best friend who she went to cake decorating school with, made the wedding cake for her. I did not have to worry about a suit because I had plenty to wear, thanks to my Auntie Ann, and I was not even excited about the damn wedding, because I knew she was marrying the Devils advocate, but she could not see, that she was about to become the bride of Chucky. When the ceremony began I tried to hold in my tears, but God would not let me, because as soon as she said I Do, tears just came barreling out of my eyes as if they were saying "If she only knew"!

Chapter Six

"ARE YOU BREATHING?"
EXHALE!

One evening when my Mother and I were coming home, my cousin noticed that the back kitchen curtain was blowing outwards, and she turned to my Mother saying "Auntie I think your window is open". Instantly my Mother immediately began to panic, and as soon as we turned the corner she jumped out of the car and ran into the house to see why the kitchen window was open. When we left that morning everything was locked up and closed, and She was puzzled as if the expression on her face was saying "What the hell is going on", so when she went into her room to take off her coat she noticed that her TV was missing, and when I went into my room to hang up my coat I noticed that all of my suits that my Auntie bought me for church was missing. That devastated me the most to see my suits gone, and at that moment I ran and told her what I noticed, and instantly she followed me to see it for herself. Some other things were missing, and instead of her calling the police, she calls him, and ask him "what was going on", and I gathered by the way she was talking to him, that he was pretending like he did not know what was going on, interesting because from that point on he never showed back up to the house for a while, and when he did all he could tell my Mother was that he had his nephew over, and a some of his other relatives, and that when they left everything was fine.

I found that hard to believe; because there was no broken window and the locks on the front doors was not even tampered with, so who ever did it did it in a way to make it seem like someone had broken in the house.

From that point on my Mother woke the hell up, ("At least I though she did"), and ended up divorcing his ass, but what behooves me is that he ended up going to jail, for what? I do not know, and I could not understand why she would go and see him in jail and take me along with her, after all the damage he had done.

When my aunt found out about my suits being gone she was pissed, and from that point on she did not buy me anything else New to wear too church, and that hurt me, because I no longer had a suit or nothing that was descent enough to wear to wear too Church, and my Mother did not even make a effort to go and replace what was gone, and what was most important to me, which was my Sunday's best.

I mean every suit of mine was gone, and they had the nerve to take my navy blue suit, which was my Usher's uniform, they could have at least left my uniform. I don't think that who ever was going to receive the stolen goods, was going to walk up in any church and join the Usher board, so I ended up going to church wearing what I had left, which was basically the clothes I had to wear too School, I was mad and upset because I was not able to Usher anymore.

One day in the midst of me cleaning, I had found in the closet which was located across from my room, a big clear bag that was hidden, and buried underneath some stuff and in it was a bunch of tiny clear capsules with blue tops, which was filled with powdery like substance. I had no clue too what it was, and I know it was the spirit of the Lord, because I had since enough to throw the bag in the trash, and from that moment I never once mentioned a word to anyone, not even my own Mother, and I held in everything that I am writing to you, at this very moment.

Eventually we ended up moving, all because she did not want to be in the apartment anymore, for the simple fact that we had a land Lord who was a Slum Lord, and did not want to fix anything, and who would just walk into your house whenever he damned pleased. I did not like him and whenever he did come to fix something I would follow him throughout the house because he had this untruthful look about him, and the only decent thing he ever did was to install a glass sliding shower door. In the interim of us moving, we went to go and stay with another family member for a brief moment, and ended up finally moving to Seaver St. in Dorchester Ma, and in June that year I mainstreamed from Knights Children Center (The Home for Little Wanderers), into another alternative Day School Program. The Case Management Team saw a need for me to continue on in special needs treatment, and thought it was not a good idea for me to return to public school.

July 1987; here I am at the Edna Stein Academy in Brookline Ma; I found it to be very difficult, adjusting to a new and unfamiliar place, and trying to make new friends was the hardest part, because from day one I was already labeled as a homosexual. The only thing that made things a little bit better for me, was the fact that some of the people that I knew from KCC transferred to this school, and also knowing that a former member of the Kelly Choir #2, a choir in which I once sung with, attended this school, and I was glad to know that she knew who I was, even though I was not a very good fan of hers (Lol). **"SOMEHOW, WE GET THROUGH IT"**, and that is what I am saying to myself as I'm writing this book, eventually I was able to make some new friends of my own; I mainly hung out with the girls because I felt more comfortable with being around them. I had some male friends who new of my lifestyle, and I'm pleased to say that none of them judged me, or called me out of my name, even when they were upset with me. We did have our Edna Stein bullies, who were insecure of themselves because they always thought that I was looking at them, in a way as if I wanted them, if they only knew, that I was looking at them to let them know, that no matter what they had to say about me, I was not going to let them move my mountain. I did not show them fear, because that's what bullies do, they intimidate you in a way for you to fear them, like Dr. Charles Hayes once said "We have nothing to fear but fear itself".

I was twelve; going on thirteen, and the classes were much more different than they were at the other school. At this school you got the privilege of switching classes for each subject. The classes were made up of different age groups, and the only class that was really different that I noticed, was the math class, because people were on different levels of math, and it was difficult to try to teach everyone the same arithmetic, due to our disabilities in learning. I found myself not getting along with some of the teachers, for the simple fact that, I noticed how they would show favor to some of the older adolescence. I did not like the fact that they treated some of us different, I guess this was the kind of treatment you would receive for being the new kid on the block, and often times the older adolescence would do things in class to get the other person in trouble, and of course the teacher would believe them over what you had to say to defend yourself from getting into trouble for something you did not do!.

A lot of times defending yourself did not help the situation any, because it only made matters worst for you. You would end up getting angry, and frustrated, too the point where you would have to act out, in an out of control manner, and be the one to be stuck in the office doing writing assignments for something you did not do. Depending on your behavior, and how bad it was, could sometimes cause you to be out of the program, or even suspended from school, or stuck in an office all day, until it was time for dismissal. There was a time when I got on the bus, and something transpired between me and the bus monitor that mad me upset, and I remember me saying too her, that her baby look just like one of those flying monkeys from the movie called the Wiz, and in fact it did, and from that day forward we never saw her again, and she looked like one of those Crack Mothers, who was on welfare, and did not have a clue about what it is to be a bus monitor,

Thank You! Jesus, because she did not have any respect for any of us riding the bus.

There was one particular teacher that I did not care much for, and I know the bible teaches us to love our enemies, but I hated her with a passion. Being around her reminded me of that old gospel record, titled, "I've been picked out, too be picked on", the both of us bumped heads all the time, In and Out of the class room, and there was an incident that took place between the both of us, that made me angry, and devastated at her, and I turned around, and told her that I was going to rip her fucking baby out of her stomach. She was not the first, or the last teacher I threatened. What made me angrier with her is the fact that she ended up pressing charges against me, and if she had of left me alone the first time; she would not have had to go to the extremes of taking legal action. She did it because she thought it was her way of teaching me a lesson, and what she failed to realize, is that no weapon form against me shall prosper, because I know that God knew what I was dealing with, and how I had to stand up for myself against the wicked ones. This particular teacher was not one for minding her own business, and from that point on she did not feel comfortable being around me, and it's a shame that you have to go to certain extremes to show people that you mean business in order for them to leave you the fuck alone, and some of them just have heads like fucking rocks, because she continued with her foolishness, so whenever we were together in and out of class, another teacher had to be present, because she was nervous and scared of me, ("I had to get my Glauc, so she can get got") "Thank You Madea", for teaching me on how to get my gotters.

I learned a lot of my life skills being at ESA & KCC, there were times where the school took a bunch of us on a field trip to Charles St. Jail, which is now known as the Nashua St. House of Corrections. The purpose of this field trip was to teach us what will happen if you were to break the law, and Madea would have done a better job! There was a name for this program; (Scared Straight) and what was I supposed to be scared about, because God is the master planner, and I have learned that no matter what comes, and what goes, I am in his hands, no matter what these teachers tried to teach nothing worked, because God is the master teacher, and if you are not of God, and not doing things by his spirit, you will not be able too move mountains. We were not the only School that participated in the Jail Break program, and often times you would see it being commercialized on Television.

While we were waiting in the auditorium for the guest inmate to come out to speak with us, I was talking amongst some of my peers, and shortly thereafter here comes the inmate along with one of the Correction Officer. When I ever looked up to see that it was my own Cousin, I immediately hide my face in awe, because I was too embarrassed, and if I could have only died for ten minutes. I then turned to my friend girl who was sitting next to me, and told her what I had discovered about the guest speaker. I told her that he was my cousin, and for some reason or another she felt as though I was lying. She immediately told the teacher, and of course, the one who I did not get along with, what I had said. The teacher then took it upon herself to interrupt the guest speaker, and asked him if he was related to me in front of the whole class. Well didn't she feel stupid, because she made a Ass out of herself, like Madea would say "Girl you are messy as hell", and blessed are the Piece Makers, Smith and Wesson" because that's what I needed at that very moment, a Piece Maker. My cousin then looked directly at me and acknowledges the fact that I was related to him, and he had the nerve to tell me to come and sit up front as if he had authority over me. So I did; and from that point on he went on and told the group how he use to whip my ass, I chuckled, and looked at him as him being an Ass Hole, because I was trying to figure out, when and how, did he whip my Ass. I was never really around him, and he was into hanging in the streets doing all kinds of bad things, selling drugs and robbing folks, and using IV needles to inject Heroin, like some of the other family members I know. He never once said to them how he would call me all kinds of horrible names, and how much of a faggot and sissy I was. See people have a way of trying to make them selves look good in front of others. I always "say", be careful of what you do to others, because one day it will all come back to bite you in the Ass. Whenever I was at my Uncles house he was never around, and neither did he attend family functions, and this is the same cousin who told me to stop looking at his Dick at my Cousin wedding, when we were in the rest room. I guess this was his way of showing off his masculinity, and it makes me wonder who is really trapped in the closet, and why would he say some shit like that, he can't be that secure about his sexuality, and makes you wonder, what is really going on behind those prison walls, I questioned myself, and asked myself, "was he somebody's Bitch". Quieted as it is kept, there are some men in the family, and women who I know is trapped in the closet, and some family members are married or dating, men and women who I know is living a doubled life, see what people don't realize, is that people of my gender can pick up on others, and in every family there is a male who's name should have been Peaches, and a women who should have been called Butch. I think back to the time when we were giving my niece In Law her baby shower, and I remember her daughter who was only two years old, and what she said too my ex spouse, which is her great uncle, "Hi Auntie", see that little girl was not stupid, and the more they kept trying to correct her in saying Uncle, the more she kept calling it for what she saw, "Auntie" (Out of the mouths of babes).

I was thirteen years old, and not only did I receive verbal abuse from him, I also experienced a great deal of it from other blood relatives, who constantly ask how I am doing by word of mouth. To those who are inquiring, and if you are reading this book, it should clearly speak through your hearts, that's if you have one, on how I am doing. I know that a lot of you do not have my best interest in heart, and this speaks also for so-called friends, and especially too my ex spouse who is still confused on what he is at the age of fifty-something, and has not accomplished anything in life, but how to be a manipulator, and take and borrow money from people in order too feed his drug habit, and don't have a conscious mind of paying the individual back, or what he has done to others in his past relationships. They say; if you do it to your own Mother, you will do it to everyone else, **("You Will Understand It Better By and BY")**. He also sits on a pulpit like his shit don't stank, and tries to make everyone think that he has changed his life style, when in fact he don't know what a piece of pussy look like, He was the bitch in the marriage, and he was the one that was on the bottom, and I was the one that was on top, **("I'M Not Going Mad, I'm Just Coming Into Myself")**, you don't really know a person until you have actually have lived with them, and I must say he is a weak willed individual, no wonder his mother was so scared and nervous, and wondering who was going to take care of his sorry ass when she went home too glory, a mother knows best, and he is one big mother fucking Boo-Boo, or better yet, "a oops baby", as one of his nieces would say.

I do not deal with my family to this very day of my life because all of the scares, and verbal, and mental abuse they have put me through, and being around them only brings back bad memories. I had a uncle who was mean and surly, and every time when I would come over to his house to see my cousin Rayton (Rest In Peace), or just to visit, he would always tell me to go home you fucking sissy, and his eyes were like a fire red as if he was the devil in disguise. The only thing that was missing was his horns and his long pitch fork, I have nothing nice to say about him and his boys, who also put me through some mental pain along with the rest of his male grandchildren for one exception, Rayton (Rest In Peace), and who was always there to defend me Thank You!!!. Pastor Hurt once said, "Stay away from folk who take you out of the spirit of God", and that is what I do. These people have now become strangers to me, I do not know who they are, and when I see them, I treat them as if they are strangers on the streets. They never included me in anything that they did, I was just lost without any body to play with or talk too, and being the only child was not easy, and I would not have been if my Egg Donor did not abort her other children, makes me wonder if I was supposed to be here or not, and guess this is why I don't have any brothers or sisters. I have come to realized, that I'm not the only child anymore, I am Gods child, and I have many other Brothers and Sisters who are in Christ Jesus who walk not after the flesh but after the spirit. "Again I say" I Thank God, for my Cousin Rayton (Rest in Peace) because he was the only one who stuck up for me when I was being bullied by other family members, and did not treat me any different. In fact; he did use to tease me, but in a good way, because there was a kid who lived on my Uncles street that I used to like, and whenever that kid would come outside, he would always say to me, your Boyfriend is outside, what's interesting is that this kid ended up becoming a Residential student at KCC shortly after I had mainstreamed into being a day student.

Chapter Seven

My Mother at this time was in transition of receiving welfare, and trying to obtain a job, until the day she was called to go and work for the MBTA (Massachusetts Bay Transportation Authority). She was happy when she received that job, and I was happy for her, because it was a good job that paid her well, and I use to walk around and brag about it, because I was so happy to tell people that my Mother worked for the T. While we were living on Seaver St., I continued on attending church at Southern Baptist, until the day I went to a banquet that was held at one of my other Aunts Church, which was not to far from the church I was attending.

While I was at this banquet, this Choir got up too sing, and I was so amazed at how this choir sung, and after the banquet was over I was introduced to this women by the named of Sis Landers. Sis Landers was the President and overseer, of the choir, and committee that was sponsoring the banquet.

My Aunt also served on this committee, but she was not apart of the choir, but she was the one who introduced me to this women who invited me to join her choir. I did not think I could join her choir because it was against church rules and regulations that you had to be a member of that church in order to serve on any auxiliary, and me having the desire to sing and direct the choir I did not know what too do in order too take part. So I went with the flow and started singing with her choir and eventually I found out that her choir was not apart of the church at all, and that her choir was a community choir that she designed, and put together herself. This choir was made up of many different families and age groups, and I grew close to Sis, Landers, and I even expressed to her how I liked directing the choir, and singing lead (The bible tells us, be ready and steadfast and unmovable always abounding in the work of the Lord).

I never would have thought that she would put me out there to actually direct and sing leads to songs, and not only that, she allowed me to bring songs to the choir as well as others, and No! I was not the only director or lead singer. This choir was truly like a family because she provided transportation for all us to attend rehearsals and outside engagements. Sometimes Bro. Landers would have to make two trips picking us up, and believe me when I tell you, we were not the best singing choir but through it all we gave God the praise in and out of tune.

This woman was phenomenal in all that she did for the choir, and for people personally, she gave what she could, and if she had you had it, often times she would take the choir out to eat for Ice cream after rehearsals, and every year we would have our annual Christmas party at the Ground Round. Every other year she would purchase new robes for our Anniversary, and everywhere we went to sing we were in Robes, one thing I can say is that none of us had to pay for our own robes, because she paid for them herself, and she was one of those people who believed in uniformity. We had two Musicians who played for us out of the two rehearsals we had throughout the week, the only difference between the two Musicians, was the fact that one only played the Piano, and the other one played the Organ.

After being with this Choir for so long I decide to become a member of that church, because it was bigger and there was a lot more to do. I joined the Junior Choir, and continued to serve as a Junior Usher, and when I ever joined the Junior Choir, Sis. Lander's was hardly upset with me, for what I do not know. So I left the Shield Lights Gospel Chorus for a while, until one day she had stopped in passing in the lower fellowship hall to ask me, if I was ever coming back to the choir, which threw me through a loop, and I don't recall what I might have said to her to that extent, but I did go back, because Singing and Directing the choir was my thing, and still is too this present day of my life.

When I joined the St. John's Missionary Baptist Church Junior Choir, I met this girl by the name of Laverne, who in fact was the president at the time. We became the best of friends from that point on, and somehow another I grew attached to her. We talked a lot on the phone with one another at first, and then I started going over her house to visit, and hang out with her, and I was privileged to meet her Mother and Father, as well as her brothers, and one of her brothers happens to be her fraternal twin. She treated me like a human being, and never once did she talk bad about me or past judgment on me; and neither did she ever deceive me, knowing that she knew I was Gay. Often times when I was around her and her straight male friends, I would tell her what I thought about them as far as looks, and if they were trapped in the closet themselves LOL. I know some of them felt uncomfortable around me, because I could sense the feeling of them being uncomfortable. Laverne never once sugar coated the fact that I was gay to anyone, and she would tell them the truth about my status quote, but she did in a way to say to them yes this is what it is, and he is still my friend, no matter what, Thank you! Laverne.

Her father was the nicest person you could have ever meet; he is a man that is humbled, and always speaking to any and everyone, with a smile on his face, it did not matter to him what you were, and often times when he was available to pick up Laverne after rehearsals, he would also give me a ride home, and the majority of the time I would take the bus or get a ride from the family that lived across the street from me, who attended the same church. Laverne and I never really argued, and I find her to be a beautiful looking woman, I admire her very much, because she is a humbled person and she is not one to pass judgment on anyone, at least not in my presence.

Eventually Laverne and her parents moved from Dorchester to Randolph Ma, and one thing I can say, is that I admired her family; they were a family that attended church as a whole, I use to sometimes sit and imagine what it would be like if I had a family like hers. When Laverne moved to Randolph I was devastated, because I did not think I was going to ever see her again, and the year that she moved to this town was the year that she decided she was not going to be the Choir President after being nominated again for Re-Election. After a while she did not attend rehearsals much because of the commute, and not only that, she had a part time job, and was doing her own thing. Laverne grew up on me and signed herself into the Army reserve, and although we may have lost contact with another, God always had a way of bringing us back together, and even to this very moment of my life. It was a Friday afternoon when I ran into her again, and I believe it was at Ashmont station when I saw her, I don't recall what I was doing that day, and where I was going, but I was just so happy to see her and I did not want to leave here presence, I know that I did not have much to do, but to go to rehearsal later on that evening, and it was early in the afternoon when we saw each other.

I was surprised to see her, and when I did I walked over to where she was standing, waiting for the #240 bus too Randolph, she looked at me as if she was In a state of shock herself, and the next thing I knew I was on the bus heading to Randolph with her.

When we got off the bus to walk down the street to her house, she realized that she did not have her Mothers eye liner pencil, and began to panic because she could not find it in her Pocket Book. When we got to the house, she gave me a tour of what the house looked liked inside and out, and I must say the house was like a dream come true.

I could tell that they were still in the process of moving, because all the boxes were not unpacked, and Miss Mary did not have the house decorated like she did on Longfellow Street, by what I saw you could tell it was going to look like a Masters Piece when it was completed, and in fact it ended up looking like what I had imagined, and who would have ever thought to put ceramic Jaguars on the roof, and ceramic Lions that sat on pedals stools at the end of the driveway.

After the tour was over she continued to back track steps, to see if she could find what was lost, and after several attempts of trying to find what was lost, we ended up leaving the house to go back up to the center of town to buy a new one. Laverne was so distraught, and broken over a simple little thing, but I guess it was not that simple because she took something that did not belong too her, and if you ever saw what her Mother looked like, you would automatically know that she did not take any shit, She was a sharp dressing woman, in and out of her MBTA uniform.

Her nails was as long as the nose of that character on the box of Froot Loops, and you would have thought that she was married too Mr. T, because of the way she wore her gold jewelry around her neck, and she had a ring for every finger, her hair was always looking sharp. I use to be scared that one day somebody was going to rob her while she was at work, but by the grace of God, no one ever did.

Laverne did not end up finding the exact color eye pencil to replace the one she lost, so we ended up going back to her house, and by the time we got back it was too late for me to go to rehearsal, because it was past 6:30pm, and her dad ended up coming home, and as I was about to leave, he offered me a ride up to the center of town, so that I could get on the bus.

One Saturday when I was at home, and bored out of my mind, I decide to take it upon myself, too go and see Laverne, but at first I hesitated in going, because I did not have her phone number to call, to see if she was going to be home, and the fact that I did not have much money to take the public transportation, but for some reason, the thought of her was heavy on my mind, and I had to go and see about her. When I finally arrived to her house I was scared to ring the bell, because I did not want her to be mad at me for not calling her first, I ended wandering around her house, ducking and hiding in and out of the bushes to see if someone was going to come out, and I did this for about a good half hour, and finally I had enough courage to go and ring the bell, and when I did, her Dad answered the door, and invited me in. when he opened the door, and invited me in, that's when he told me that Laverne was not home, and no one knew where she had gone, so I waited a while, and finally she called the house and spoke to her father, and he told her that I was there waiting for her. When I finally had the chance too speak with her on the phone, she yelled at me "what you doing coming by my house, you need to call me before coming over" she went on and on, ("Did she just shut me down?, "SHUT UP", "BOOF") and then finally she came to her senses, and said that she was not going to be home anytime soon. When I hung up the phone with her, I told her Dad what she had said, and once again he was nice enough to give me a ride back up to the center of town, so that I could get back on the bus to go home. Laverne never new how important it meant to me to go see her that day, I was going through some rough moments, and I just needed away to escape that day, from all the mental abuse that I was dealing with.

While living on Seaver St. I met this family that lived diagonally across the street from us who had attended the same church, and sung in the same Choir. The Mother sung in the young Adult Choir, who sung combined with the Junior Choir on 2nd Sundays, and on the fourth Sunday they sung with the Male Chorus. I was glad to have met them because it made life a lot easier in getting to and from church at times, especially on Friday nights when we had Rehearsals. I spent a lot of my time at their house when it was ok for me to come over, and sometimes I would even have dinner with them, and I was grateful for that, because there were times where I had to go without food, and no one knew, but me and Daddy God. Mrs. Moore was a Mother who worked hard and did any and everything when it came to taking care of her family, and if she was hurting inside, you would have never known, because she always had smile on her face.

There were times when she would give me a look as if she was serious, because I sometimes would crack jokes with her, and I knew right then and there too leave her alone, and trust me, I did. I enjoyed the fact that she would take me along with her as her third or fourth wheel to all of her singing engagements, Mrs. Moore did not only just sing with the Kelly Choir #2, she was also a member of a local group, which sung in and around the City of Boston, who called themselves the Owen Sisters.

There was a woman who sung in the group that caught my attention every time I would see them sing, this woman had a passion for singing, because I noticed, and felt her spirit while she was singing, as she walked the floors of the churches with the microphone in one hand pointing to the people with the other. What tickled me about her and the rest of them, were the fact that they wore something that looked like white snow flakes on the top of their heads and another thing that I noticed about her, is that she was the only one out of the group who was happy, and sincere about singing for the Lord, until the day I met her and found out who she really was and what she was all about, (YOU WILL UNDERSTAND IT BETTER BY AND BY).

It is very true that we need to be aware of our facial expressions, and body language, when we are doing Gods work, because you do not know who is watching you, if you are doing Gods work with a negative spirit, you are not going to be able to Minister to others who may be hurting.

One day while Mrs. Moore's Children and I were outside playing, I ended up getting into a fight with one of the kids that lived in my building on the second floor; this kid was nothing but trouble, as well as the rest of his siblings. I was never one to start or instigate a fight, I did not like fighting, and there comes a time when you have to go to the extreme to earn respect for yourself, and at this point I was really sick and tired of being called a fagot. Ever since that wonderful day my soul has been satisfied, "yes with Jesus" because he gave me the strength to defend myself. I whopped his ass, to the point where I ended up drawing blood, and when I did, I scared myself, because I didn't know my own strength. I could not stand the fact of being bullied, and it was time for me to stop running and Kick Ass.

There was one evening when my Mother had sent me to the store, to purchase her a pack of cigarettes for her, and on the way back from the store, I had noticed a group of teenage boys walking in a pack, and right then and there I stopped.

I started thinking of another way to go home, because I had sensed trouble and I was scared, because I did not know if they were going to bother me.

So my subconscious mind told me to go ahead, and walk past them, and when I did they stopped me, and immediately they checked my pockets and all they found was the cigarettes that I just had purchased for my Mother, and decide to take those. I remember telling them to leave me alone, and I was too scared to scream for help, and before I knew it, they just started beating on me for no apparent reason with a golf club.

I was too scared to even fight back, because there were too many of them, and the fact of them being bigger and older than me, and not knowing if they were armed. When they finally released me to go, I ran home like Road Runner from Bugs Bunny. When I got home my Mother did not show no concern of what had just happened, all she was concerned about was her cigarettes, and when she found out that I did not have them she got even angrier at me, She started yelling and screaming, telling me that I should have whooped their Ass, "ok, did she think I was Bruce Lee, or better yet Jackie Chan".

I was devastated to hear that come out of her mouth; I did not know what to do at that point but to go in my room and go to bed. I thank God because I could have been killed that night, and I wonder? How she would have felt, or what she would have said, if the Police were ever to knock on her door, too tell her that I was killed.

Nothing I ever did was good enough, even me being a honor roll student, and she was not even concerned with what was going on with me, or how I felt inside, because she always had a man around her, married or not, and was never home. I thank God for one of her male friends, because at times he stepped in with making sure we had food too eat, and buying me a few pieces of clothing when she was not able too.

This man sometimes would bring KFC to the house, which was one of my favorite places to eat, and by him doing what he could, made me happy, and often times there would be leftovers, but if I ate it without permission, I got yelled at, and called all kinds of nasty names, because she thought I was being selfish and inconsiderate. She knew that there was nothing in the house to eat at times, except for the surplus food she would get from the food banks, and some of it was not healthy to eat, and did she forget that I was a child, and that it was her responsibility to take care of me.

It was during spring or early summer when my cousin came with his son to visit us from Atlanta, and when I found out that he was going to stay with us I was happy because finally I was going to have some company. In the meanwhile I was trying to figure out where these two was going to sleep, because we did not have much for furniture, and what we did have was half way descent, considering that it was donated from an outside agency, Like Salvation Army.

She had lost a lot of our things because of moving, and the only things that we had that I remember, was my Black and white television that I had won selling candy at the Mattahunt School, and the Bunk Bed set that she had bought me when we were living on Winter St. I ended up being creative in turning my bunk bed in to a single bed with two mattresses, because I did not see any use in setting up the top bunk, and the fact that there were pieces missing.

When my Cousin finally came, he noticed that there was nothing to eat in the house, and proceeded to ask me why there was no food, and me being so embarrassed I could not answer any of his questions, and little did he know that there were times when she wouldn't come home for days, and that there were days I would come home hungry having to have to fend for myself, finding what ever I could put together to eat. I had no clue too what my Mother was doing with her money, and the food stamps that, but things were starting to become a little strange to me, and there were times when she did go shopping, and for some strange reason, she would accuse me of giving food away to the neighbors, and the kids outside, and she use to tell me that she was not going to buy any more food, so I guess this was her way of making me suffer. Her behavior was on going, to the point where I just started accepting things for what it was, because I was a child, and I was too scared and embarrassed to ever open up too tell anyone, especially family members, to let them know what was going on, and the fact that I was labeled to be a liar, and they would not have believed any thing I would have said. Everyone thought I was this kid, who just went around and told lies, it is sad when adults don't learn to listen to children until it is too late in the game.

When my cousin found out that there was no food to eat, and that my Mother did not provide adequate hospitality, he got on the phone and called my Aunt in Mattapan Ma, to explain to her what was going on. After he had made the arrangements to go and stay with her, I showed him where the corner store was, so that he could go and by a half gallon of milk, and a box of cereal for him and his son to eat, until someone came to pick him up, and take him to Auntie's house. When he finally left to go, I was heart broken, and wanted to go too, because I was lonely and had no one to play with, as well as being hungry. When she finally returned after being missing for a while, she asked me where did he go, and I told her, and I distinctly remember her calling my Aunt to see what was going on, and when she did my Aunt went off on her, and told her about herself and my Mother got mad, and said to herself, Fuck It. I don't know what was actually said, but I know it was not something she wanted to hear. What was going on in her mind at this time, I did not know, but who in their right mind invite people to stay with them, without any kind of hospitality and knowing that they have issues within themselves.

Chapter Eight

Eventually the Moore Family ended up Moving into a duplex house in Roxbury, and shortly thereafter we ended up moving to 185 Walnut Ave Apt 1 & 1/2. The advantage of moving to this location was great, because I was in walking distance to the Church and my Aunt's house, which also lived on Walnut Ave, but at #49.

I was able too continue my relationship as well as being able too walk to the Moore's Family house; and the only thing that really changed, was the fact that my School bus had to pick me up at another location. It was about a year or so, after we had moved to this location, when I met my Mother and her Co- worker at work one day after school, and some way or another we ended up at my Aunts house on Cheney St. in Roxbury Ma,.

While we were all standing outside of my Aunts house on the front steps, my cousin pulled up to the front of the house, and asked my Mother if we lived in the apartment buildings on the corner of Walnut & MLK Blvd, and she responded "yes". My cousin now tells her that our building was on fire, and in return my Mother said to her, stop kidding around, and my cousin said "No Auntie I am for real", My cousin had a way of joking with people, and sometimes you did not know weather or not to take her seriously, at that moment my Mother began to panic and part her way to go and see what was really going on, and her friend who was with us went her way as well.

Well I'll be damned; it was in fact true, that our Apartment Building had caught on fire, and you could tell by the look on my Mothers face, that she was one pissed bitch. To come home to something so devastating was enough to blow any ones mind, especially having to have to deal with the general fucking public all day. My Mother had to maintain her composure, in order to find out more and in-depth details of what happened, and why?

Apparently the fire started on the second floor, in the bedroom that was right above mine, and we was not allowed too go into the building until after the fire chief gave everyone the ok that it was safe to go in, and that night we ended having to go stay in a hotel due to all the water damage that we had, and until management had the time to estimate the cost of the damages, and to decide what repairs needed to be done to all the units that were effected by the fire.

When I ever walked into our apartment, I was in a state of shock, for this was the first time ever having to go through something like this. It was devastating to see all of the water dripping from the ceiling and light fixtures; when I got to my room, I could not believe my eyes even more.

Little of what I had was ruined, and what was worst about the whole situation is that everything was filled, and smelled like smoke, now I know what it is like to be a victim of disaster, and I just want to say, "Thank you Jesus", because it could have been a lot worst, the fire could have spread throughout the entire building, but it didn't, "God Blocked It", due to the negligence of others.

The American Red Cross took good care of us with assisting us with shelter and food, and other necessities. We stayed in the Howard Johnsons hotel for a few days, and I did not go to school, and neither did my Mother attend work the next day, because of what happened. When we returned home from being displaced, we walked into a smelly smoked-defied mess, the aftermath was even worst, our clothes reeked of smoke as well as the linen, and everything else was filled with soot.

The electricians had to re- wire all the light fixtures, and maintenance had to come in and re-paint, and shampoo the carpet. We were not even able to watch television, because they were filled with water, and we had to place them on the back porch upside down to dry out. I thank God, because it was late spring, going into the summer, and we had some warm days, that allowed us to wash up everything in the house and hang them out on the clothes line that my Mother had made on the back porch. We had a dryer but that thing broke, and it just sat in one area on display taking up space.

My Mother had that washer and dryer set, ever since I was a toddler and I thank God for the washer not being broke, but able to wash our clothes, the maintenance department provided us with some special laundry detergent solvent, which was given to them by the American Red Cross, and there was even some in the care package bags that the Red Cross had given us. The more the better and the stuff work pretty well, it did help to eliminate the smoke that was in our clothes. It took us almost the entire summer to readjust and put things back into perspective, and when it came time for me to plug up my television I was scared, because I did not know if it was going to explode or electric cute me, "thank you Jesus", for those two twins, Grace and Mercy, because it brought me through, while I began to plug the television back into the socket.

December of 1988 I turned fourteen years old, and was glad that I finally turned fourteen years of age; I was now able to get working papers and work to earn money for my own pocket. My school had a summer contract with a company called ABCD, who provided summer jobs for those that were eligible, in and around the city of Boston. My school had a contract with them, that allowed a few of us to work in and around the school during the summer sessions, and Applications had to be submitted by a certain deadline to be approved and processed, and some people did not get accepted, either because they were apart of the program the following year, or because there was only limited jobs that were available. When the summer program ended, I wanted to continue working, and I did, I was provided working papers from my school, and had obtained a job working for Mc Donald's in the Lafayette mall Downtown Boston.

I was grateful and blessed that my school allowed me to continue to work after school hours, and for the fact of me being able to take the public transportation to get to work right after school. That meant that I did not have to ride the little short blue bus home, and be late for work. On days that I did not have to work I still took the bus home, all because I felt independent in doing so, and I was sick and tired of riding the bus with all those farmers. Some mornings I would miss the bus purposely, just to come to school on my own, and often times they got upset, because I did not get permission to come to school on public transportation.

About six months after working for McDonalds; I was fired, because the store manager said that I had to many overages, and in fact I did, I found ways on how to beat the cash register, I was devastated when that happened, I did not know what to do with myself for a while, and I had no choice, but to tell the school that I was no longer working, and that meant that I had to go back to riding the short bus home again, because I did not have money to take the public transportation anymore. Like the song writer once said "We Fall Down, But we get up" and I did, very much so, I started in the early spring, the following year, working for a guy who owned a skate shop on Green St. in Jamaica Plain Ma, who had a contract with the Boston Herald to sell news papers, on various corners in and around the community, in the early am.

I appreciated this man; because while we were out there on the busy streets hustling news papers, he often stopped by to check on us, and to make sure that we were not running out of papers to sell, and to collect money when our money holder was filled. He made sure that we were safe and warm, especially during the winter season, and often times he would take us out for breakfast on the weekends at his own expense. Sometimes when he would pick us up after we were done, he often had donuts, coffee and juice for us in the van. He always picked me up in time enough for me to return home to get ready for school, and be on time for when the little blue short bus came. This job did not last for long, because it was getting too cold, and I was tired of standing on the corner in the middle of winter selling news papers.

During this period of my life things began to turn into the ultimate worst, it was like God removing blinders off my eyes at such a young age to see, and to notice things more clearly, and what was going on in and around me. It was early in the day when my Mother came home from work, and by the looks on her face I could tell that something was wrong with her.

When I asked her what was wrong, she told me that she had an accident with the bus, and did not really want to talk about it much, and ever since that day she did not return to work for the MBTA, and she became more and more depressed in her spirit, and things started to shift and turn in both of our lives. She did manage to obtain other employment else where, which did not last very long, and eventually she ended up on receiving Welfare again.

At this point I was lost, lost to the fact that I could not understand what was going on, and why my cousins would often times come over our house late in the midnight hours, as well as other friends of hers, and there were times when I would awake to go to school, or either to church, to only find them in the house locked up in her bed room.

That disturbed me because I did not know what to do or say at this point, and what direction to go into, I kept myself busy in doing other things, either going to Choir Rehearsals, or Church, and too the Boy's & Girls Club of Roxbury Ma, and sometimes I even found myself in Mattapan at Auntie Dottie's house hanging out with Kenyon and Kyran.

There were nights while I was asleep, and I would either be awakened by her or others that was in the house, all because they would be in the kitchen area, where my room was located, and My Mother sometimes would close my room door, so that I could not see or hear what was going on, and little did she know, I was not asleep, and at times I got up and peeked through the crack of the door, to see what was going on, and often times I noticed someone standing at the stove boiling water in this small silver pot, that I would use to boil my eggs in.

There was one particular night when I was asleep, and suddenly, I was awakened by her, and when I ever got up out of my deep sleep to look up at her, all I saw was this woman whose eyes looked like Uncle Festers eyes on the Adams Family, and this was not the first time I had been awakened, and I could not figure out how this women would be up all night looking like she just drunk a case of red bull. This was scary, because I did not know what the hell was going on, so I asked her what did she want, and she told me to give her my Gold ring that I had on my finger, and I said "what", and she said "yes", I need it, and I asked her again for what. By then she could not answer me, and as I became more resistant in telling her no, she became more manipulative.

Finally I gave in, and gave it to her, all because she said that someone was after her, and right then I knew what she wanted it for. She wanted it for drugs, and she took something that was of value to me to satisfy her own needs. I worked hard for that ring, and what made that ring so special, is because it was my first piece of gold jewelry that I had bought for myself while I was working, and it had my initials engraved on the top. From that point I lost total respect for her, I cried like hell that night, and I did not even see her for a few days after that, and there were many days like this prior. What made matters worst is that whenever some of my cousins was over smoking crack with her, I had to watch and baby sit their kids, Hmmm, and if they only new who they were. Now I know where those crack capsules came from that I found on Alpine St. in the closet, and what I can't understand is why did she get high with her nieces and nephews?, and who taught who how to smoke crack first, this is not being a positive roll model, and setting a good example for the next generation. I tell you the truth, these crack Mothers are something else, "why people want to smoke crack?", "crack is whack", "don't weed get them high enough", "look", "I'm high, and I ant smoke no crack", "and further more, I'm in the midst of writing", "conjunction, junction, what's your function?"

I always knew when she would receive her checks and food stamps, because she would always be missing for days, and often times she would come back with some food stamps, and send me to the store to buy some food, and other times she would come back home broke, with no food stamps, why? Because she would have spent it all on drugs, and when she would come down from her high I got the brunt end of her negative attitude.

This woman was so mean to me, and At times I would be put on punishment either for giving food away, or for little stupid shit that I did not even do. Her way of punishing me, was that I could no longer attend church and choir rehearsals, because I was doing the work of the Devil, I was called a hypocrite and a liar, and other derogatory names as well.

It hurt me not being able to attend church, for that was like therapy for me, even though I may not have understood, or was able to comprehend what that Pastor was preaching about, I still had the desire to go. What I got out of church, and what made me happy was the fact that I sung in the choir and enjoyed singing, when it came time for choir anniversaries, or anything that was positive, that I was apart of, did not interest her at all. I received no support, in fact; I was even more so happy to see my Aunt who would sometimes come back out for afternoon programs sitting in the congregation whenever there was something going on that I was involved in.

Even when I made the effort to invite her, neither did she make an effort to get up on Sunday mornings to attend church with me. When she ever told me that I could not go to church anymore, I did not pay her any attention, and disobeyed her will, and obeyed God's will, and went anyways because he was speaking through my heart, and my desire was to get up and go, because the spirit of the Lord was upon me, (Psalms 27:10 Says "Though my Father and my Mother forsake me, the Lord will receive me"). I was not about to let her take something that meant allot away from me, and neither was God, He was connected with me all this time, but I did not realize it, until I just wrote what I just said. She did it because she knew church meant something to me, and what parent does that to a child? Telling them that they can not go to church, (she was possessed by Beelzebub! the prince of demons).

I kept asking myself; was this right? And when I did go against her will and did what I damned pleased, she did not like it, so she started taking house keys from me, leaving me stranded to the point where I would find myself at my Aunts house down the street, sitting with my uncle or wandering the streets at other peoples houses until she got home, and sometimes she did not come home, and I was left in the streets. So I got smart, and before I would leave the house, I use to leave the bathroom window unlocked which was located on the back porch, hoping that she would not find out. When she did come home, it did not dawn on her as to how I got into the house, and She played this game for a while, and sometimes I did loose my keys, but not purposely, and that was another reason for her not giving me another set, because she was so paranoid to the fact, that she thought that who ever would have found my house keys knew where we lived, and she would go to the extremes in getting the locks changed.

I went to school and church holding all of this pain inside of me, even the fact that I was molested by my cousin who is now diseased, and the only thing that saved me that day was the fact that my Aunt walked in the room after he had already ejaculated all over me, I was devastated, and did not know what too do, think, or say at such a young age, and Still to this day my Aunt has kept it a secret, and I am now glad that I can open up and reveal this devastating secret. There is another family member, who was a victim of his behavior of molestation, and I'm glad to know that I'm not alone. I could not understand why my Aunt kept this a secret, and one of my Aunts, who I was able to open up and explain to her what had happen to me, told me that she was probably too embarrassed to tell anyone, "still that is no excuse" because as you can see, secrets only destroy you, and eventually they will come to surface, and people need to know what is going on, so that they can protect their children from being victims as well. She new her son had issues, but yet she did not seek to find him help, Madea could not have said it any better, we are often taught, that what goes on in the house, stays in the house, "BULLSHIT", "if what's going on in the house is hurting me, I'm going to tell someone so that I can get help".

It was not until I found out that my cousin had passed, when I finally opened up to my birth Mother, and told her what happened to me, and when I told her she was devastated her self, and mad, and could not understand why her sister kept what happened to me from her, right then and there she realized that she could not trust her own family, and was more saddened, because she protected their children when they were younger, and in her care, and why couldn't they not have done the same for hers?. My Birth Mother opened up to me, and told me, that she was molested by her own Brother, and often times she was approached by her brother in law, but nothing happened, and all these years she has held in the pain to what has happened to her and her niece, whom shall remain nameless, because it will be devastating if my cousins knew that their Father was a molester (**"J'Korey!", "you have got to stop smoking Reefer", "I'm really afraid to hear what you have to say next", Laugh out loud, that is what I am saying to myself as I continue to write, "conjunction, junction, what's my function?"**). This family has to many secrets, and what behooves me is that they can't come together as one, and have a descent family reunion, why?, Because there is too much division going on, everyone is trying to out do one another, either in envy, hypocrisy, or seeking malicious ways to target one another, and because of the history of molestation and abuse of drugs, and alcoholism, that they use in order to hide all the pain that they have inside of them, due to generational curses. I'm so glad to know who Jesus is, because when I look at the history of drug abuse in this family, and how it has destroyed them, it makes me a stronger person to not want too ever pick up the habit, and the fact of being on that stuff destroys their minds, and they cant even remember how they have hurt loved ones by their behavior, and How they have destroyed many relationships, which take years of rebuilding because of the lost of love, and respect, and mental, and physical abuse they have caused another.

What makes matters worst is that they want to justify that smoking marijuana is just as bad, when in fact, it isn't, because it does not strip you of who you are, and make you do evil things to harm others, and if it is so bad, then why are the doctors prescribing it to people who are sick with Cancer and HIV, "conjunction, junction what's their function"?

This is why I do not go over to my Aunts house to see her as much, because it only brings back hurtful memories, people often ask why I didn't attend his funeral, and I remember saying to them, "who in there right mind is going to attend a funeral by someone who molested them", my cousin who was molested by him did, but I'm not her. People need to be more careful of the questions they ask, because often times you will hear things, that you did not intend to hear, but if you know me, and who I am, I am blunt, and I am going to tell you the truth, and how I feel, and I do not give a fat baby's Ass, who gets offended, because I have kept my mouth shut for thirty-six and a 1/2 years, and again I will say **"I'M NOT GOING MAD I'M JUST COMING INTO MYSELF"**, ("Conjunction, Junction, That's My Function"), and the fact that the truth hurts and reality sucks, and further more I do not serve a sugar coating God! ("Do you understand the words that are coming out of my mouth"?)

There were times I could not wait to get to school; because that was the only time I really had a descent meal to eat. I was blessed on the weekends, because if it was not for my Aunt and Sister Landers working in the kitchen, I don't know what I would have done for food.

Christmas of 1989, the Jones family ended up relocating from Mattapan Ma, to Peoria Arizona, I was lost when they had left, and if Auntie Dottie new what I was going through, I know that she would have taking me along with her, because she was there every time I called her to come and pick me up from the Home for little Wanderers, when I did not even want to be there, and because of the love and compassion she has for children. In fact it was not God's intentions, because he new that one day, I was going to turn this mess into a message, and my tests was going to be my testimony, because he is the only one that can give the victim the victory, and turn trials into triumph.

Chapter Nine

April of 1990, I was hit by a car on Columbus Ave, right across the street from Jackson Sq T station, and truly I thank God for his grace and mercy that day, because it was a horrifying, and for the witnesses who were there as well, what is so interesting about this, is that, half of the people that helped me knew who I was. The reason being is because they use to buy their news paper from me in the early Am, and it just so happened, that the accident took place right at that same intersection where I use too stand. One other person that was there at the scene, that I noticed, was a gentleman who attended the same church.

In a matter of seconds the police and ambulance came, and for a moment I had blacked out, because everything happened so quickly, and when I finally realized that I was in the middle of the street, I tried to get up and walk too get closer to the side walk, and realized that my leg was broken. So what I ended up doing was sliding myself backwards, with the help of others, towards the middle of the divided street, to sit on the curb, and try to gain what little conscious, I had.

When the paramedics arrived they took and strapped me down to a long hard board, and I could not make sense of that fact, of why they were strapping me down. I felt like I was an escapee from a mental hospital, I'm glad that when I came home from school, before heading out I changed my clothes, because it was devastating to lay down, in what felt like a restraint for crazy people, and too watch them cut up my clothes to get to the injury ("I must say, "I am crazy", "but not that kind of crazy"). Here I am fifteen years old, and don't have a clue to what was going on, it was all like a dream to me, and still to this day, I can say, "Gods Grace & Mercy, brought me through".

When we arrived at the Boston Children's Hospital, I was immediately rushed into the emergency room, where I received adequate attention, I must say it was nice to see people giving me some positive attention for a change, I felt like a king on a throne, but in a lot of pain. It was hours before they finally decided to unstrapped me from the board; in the meanwhile, I was asking all kinds of questions, and apparently they strapped me down, because they wanted to make sure that I did not suffer from any head trauma, or back injuries, I had to stay in this position until they took x-rays.

As the evening went on; someone finally came and rolled my incapacitated ass into the x-ray room, and after the doctors saw that I did not have any other injuries to my head and spine; they then released me from the board, "thank you Jesus!!!"

My leg was broken so bad, and because of the internal bleeding they ended up admitting me into the hospital, and it was hours before I ended up being transported to a room that was available. Finally; here come the women who should have been stripped of her parental rights along time ago, who once said to me, she was never taught how to raise a child, but little do she know, no one was giving a manual on how to raise children, and children were not born in a Matel, Parker Brothers or Milton Bradley box, and then placed on your local toy store shelf like Ken and Barbie, who came with instructions.

She came in fussing and cussing, and yelling at me in front of everyone in the ER, "If you would have stayed your ass in the house, none of this shit would have happened" in other words, she might as well had said "that's what your black hard headed ass get" instead of carrying on, in a foolish manner. Again; I say, would she have been saying that, if that car had of killed me (count your blessings). Who wanted to hear all of that, I didn't, I realized even more so at that moment, that she was selfish and inconsiderate towards me, I'm always reminded that I'm just like my sperm donor, whom she does not like, because of the things that he has done to her while she was pregnant with me, and even after I was born, I was only five years old when I saw him last, **(Dig if you will the picture, you and I engaged in a twist, how can you just leave me standing ?, Alone in a world that's so cold ?, Maybe I'm just like Mother, she's never satisfied, maybe I'm just like my Father, too bold, why do we scream at each other, this is what it sounds like when Doves Cry).**

It was embarrassing to see her come in the way she did, and how she found out, is a mystery, a mystery that

Scooby Doo would have a hard time figuring out, only Jesus can work this Out.............. What did she expect for me to do, when I did not have any one to play with, or talk too, does anyone know what it is like to be the only child? And she was never home, and if she was, she did not have any money to do anything with. It was all about her, and I wonder sometimes, if she ever receive love and attention when she was a child, or is the fact that the crack had her so messed up, too the point, where she could not focus, "somebody please tell me what was really going on.

I was in the hospital for almost about a month, because every time they went to re-set the bone, and was ready to discharge me, the bone would somehow slip out of place. I had a hard time with adjusting to walking with crutches, so what ended up happening, was that they had to order me a wheel chair for the house, which I did not use, because it was impossible to move around in.

While I was in the hospital, I even asked her to stay the night with me, and at first, she fussed and complained, but eventually she did, and woke up the next morning fussing, because she was uncomfortable.

I did not see much of her for a while, while I was in the hospital, but I thank God for the few that did take the time to come and see me, especially my Auntie, who was kind of like a Mother to me and who thought of me as her son, and one thing I can say, is that she was always been there too support, even when times were good or bad, and I always looked forward too Christmas, because I knew that she would always have a gift for me, and it meant a lot, because there were no more holidays in the Walker's household.

I even received a visit from Sis. Florence Searcy (Rest in Peace), who was the assistant supervisor of the Junior Choir, this woman of God meant a lot to me as well, because there were times where she would take me home after church with her and her daughter, and feed me, and most of the time when I would go home with her was because of the fact that we ended having to go to other churches, for afternoon programs, or even back to our home church. Even Mrs. Moore Daughter who sung on the Junior Choir came along with Jo-Ann who sung with me as well in the Shield Lights Gospel Chorus; apparently the two of them attended the same school and decided to come to see me one day, after school. I received cards and Balloons, and most of it came from the people in church, and what really touched my heart was too open up one of my cards that were signed by the entire Junior Choir.

When I was discharged to go home, I ended up still having to fend for myself, it was difficult trying to get dress, knowing that my pants leg would not go over my cast, and I was getting tired of cutting up what little I had for clothing. So I decided to wear sweat pants instead, and in fact it worked out for me, because they went on easy, and I did not have to cut them. It was a second Sunday, When I returned to church in my all white suite only to be singing again with the junior choir, but only this time with a cast on my leg. When it was time for the choir to process in, I was already in, what we called the choir box. It was odd standing up there watching and waiting for them to process in, I was kind of pissed off, because that was one of my favorite parts of being in the choir, and after offering was over, one of the deacons came into the choir stand and handed me this little manila envelope.

When I opened the envelope, there was Seventy Five dollars in it, and I could not understand why they were handing me an envelope with money in it, but now I do, it was a love offering, and I was grateful to have it, and I used the money too get me through the following week for food, and for school, and I never mentioned a word to my egg donor what I received in church that day, because it was a blessing for me, "God gives favor to whom he chooses". I was even shocked that she even drove me too church that Sunday in her school van. I thank God for Deacon Odom (Rest in Peace), because he was the one who handed me the envelope.

When I returned too school, I receive help from some of my peers and managed to get up and down the stairs on my own. Even though I had a cast on my leg, I did not let it stop me from doing what I would do normally, and eventually the doctors ended up giving me a boot, and before that I was already walking on the cast, because those crouches didn't do me any justice, like I said before **"You Can't Keep a Blessed Man Down"**.

I spent most of the summer in the cast, until August of that year, when the cast was finally removed; and shortly before the cast was removed, I received a surprised visit from my sperm donor. How he ended up finding me was because of the fact that he remembered where my Aunt lived in Mattapan Ma, and of course my Aunt called my So-Called Mother to tell her that he was in town, and where did he come from, only God knows.

All I know was that my egg donor came home with the ass hole that she had married, who had stolen all of our stuff, to pick me up in her School car, so that she could take me to see my sperm donor, seeing her x husband in the car, through me through a loop, where the hell did he come from, this was the first time I had seen this man since she divorced his ass, was she sick, or did she bump her fucking head, "Oh No" he would have gotten some bust a cap in his ass kind of care, or a beat down until he was twelve feet under, **("The height of a person, doubles the burial")**. She never did say where we were going, but as we got closer to our destination I recognized that we were going to my Aunts house.

When we finally arrived I got out of the car, and there he was sitting on the stairs talking to my Aunt and all I remember him saying was "What's up boy", with his stuttering accent. I was in a state of shock to see this six foot, seven inch, tall, and high yellow man, that wore a jerry curl, and also walked with a limp because of him having polio. I did not know what to say at that moment, too some one who I have not seen in almost ten years. I ended up spending that weekend with him while he was in town at one of the Days Inn Hotel. What made matters worst is the fact that I had to sleep in the same bed as him, "my

God", was he that cheap, or that broke that he could not up grade to a room that had double beds. It was strange, because I did not know this man, and I was uncomfortable, and if I did feel comfortable being with him, I would have never gotten any sleep, because this man snored so bad that you would have thought a bulldozer was coming to tear down the hotel. He took me shopping and out to eat that entire weekend, and I appreciated it because half of my clothes were ruined, because of the alterations I had to do to them in order for them to fit over the cast. I was in need of new clothing and shoes any ways, and see God has a way of showing up, to show out, "thank you Jesus"!!! We eventually talked; not about much of anything, I did not even bother to open up to tell him what was going on. If I did; would he have cared? No because when our visit was over he promised to send for me and to spend more time with me, and all that he had said, was nothing but lies, because he did not fulfill any of the promises that he had made to me, **(When my father and my mother forsake me, the Lord will receive me, Psalms 27:10)**.

Every time I picked up the phone to call him in Chicago where he was living at the time with his wife, I would always receive some kind of excuse, this also put a toll on me mentally, because I did not know what to do, so finally I gave up in calling him. How can some one just come into your life after all these years and make false promises, especially to a child and don't have any conscious of how it would affect them.

He was better off in keeping his high yellow ass where he was, because I was doing fine all by myself until he showed up. The Bible says you will reap what you sew, and I can attest to that, because he is know suffering, suffering to the point where he had five strokes, and now he is totally disabled in a Nursing home, and suffering from short term memory lost.

I know this; because I was just recently informed by my cousin, who is his nephew, who also has mental issues, because still I'm trying to figure out how can he be mad at me for the way I feel towards my sperm donor, although he was there for him as his uncle, but what about the children he was supposed to father, "yes, I agree, something is mentally wrong with him" because there is no comparison in the roll my sperm donor was supposed to play. We are all Actors and Actresses on a stage, but only a few get the part to play the roll.

How did I ever get in touch with my cousin? Was because of my egg donor who took it upon herself to go and search for him on Face book, and then she decided to give him my phone number without my permission, and I was also informed that I have other brothers and sisters, and that I am the third oldest child of his, (Papa was a rolling stone, wherever he laid his Dick was his home,).

I did get the chance to talk to my sperm donor on the phone, and I could tell for myself that he was sick; I really don't think he actually knew who I was, even though he said he did, and I could also tell by the way he was speaking, that his speech impairment was off, and his words slurred, and things just did not seem right. Did I feel sorry for him? No, because he made his bed, and now he has to lie in it, "Am I going to run to his rescue"? "Hell to the no", but I do forgive him, whole heartedly, and I'm going to continue on with my life, and if its Gods will, then I guess we will meet, or when I see Jesus, Amen.

One night while I was home in my room, my egg donor asked me to come into her room, for what? I did not know; and when I entered she closed the door and pulled out this envelope that was filled with money.

I asked her where did she get all of that money from, and she told me that it was my settlement money from my accident. Then I asked if I could have some of it? And she told me no, then I said to her, "well", "what are you going to do with it", and at that point she could not answer me. So the next day I did not go to school, and she had one of her male friends, who she was dating at the time, take me shopping, and off we went to Burlington Coat Factory where she only spent a good three hundred dollars on me.

I don't really know how much money was there, but I know it was a lump sum, and she blew all that money on drugs, and in bailing out my Uncle who owed the Heroin dealer money, and still to this present day he has not paid her back, or better yet me, because in all actuality it belonged to me, I was the one who suffered from being hit by a drunk driver. What is so interesting is that he suffered a stroke in, and around the month of September and October of 2010, and the doctors has cleared him to be totally disabled, and now he can't even go back to work, and now he is at the mercy of depending on others too take care of him, and it wasn't until my cousin asked me to go and do her a favor, by picking up his dirty laundry from the nursing home, where he was staying, so that she or my Aunt could wash them, is when I realized that he could not even look me in my face, because of what he had done, again I say, God has away of making your oppressor's your footstool, I even sent him plates of food home, from past cookouts that was held at my house, through my Aunt, who insisted on taking him something too eat, and that goes to show you, that you will never know where your next meal is going to come from, and pray too God that it won't be from someone who you may have done wrong.

What really puts the icing on the cake, is the fact that she was also getting high with my teacher who happened to live around the corner from where we were living at the time, and apparently she loaned her some of the money, and when she did not pay her back, she went and told the school, who ended up giving her the money back, and immediately that teacher was fired, because it was against company's policies, that teachers were not allowed to have outside personal relationships with the families, and she did. I remember going over her house a few times with my egg donor, and I was left in the living room as always, whenever she took me along with her to get high, "Oh yes" she did take places with her to get high, as if I did not know what was going on. I knew what was going on, but I did not say anything, and it was difficult enough to go to school everyday holding in what I knew. When this teacher was fired I got the brunt end of it, and I could never understood why my peers was blaming me for this teacher being fired, until the day my so-called parent told me what happened.

At first I was not surprised, because I had already knew what the deal was, but again, I was hurt, because what kind of parental guidance was she teaching me. I became even more disgusted with her, and from that moment on, I continued to hold my head up, and continued to look after me the best way I knew how. I asked her to this day, why didn't she put the money away in a trust fund? Or better yet, it would have made me happier, if she would have used it too by us some new furniture, since she claims that it wasn't a lot of money. Whatever it was, it was enough for her to buy crack, friends, and family, "what a disgrace".

The problem with this is that every time I bring it up she gets defensive, and has a hard time with facing the reality of it all, but what she does not seem to realize that I'm over all of that, and I know that God has returned to me a hundred fold, of everything the devil has robbed me of. What gets me is that she told me back in April of 2010 that the Lord told her to pay me back the money she took from me, I questioned that, and immediately prayed and asked God for guidance, and then this scripture came to me and it said, "Simon, Simon, in other words J'Korey, J'Korey, Satan has asked to sift you as wheat, but I have prayed for you, J'Korey that your faith may not fail. And when you have turned back strengthen your brothers." (Luke 22: 31) in other words, she lied on God, because she started adding up stuff that she gave to me some years ago, and began to calculate what she thought she owed me, and when she ever told me that she only owed me a thousand dollars, I stopped, and said to myself this is not of God, this is the trick of the enemy, in fact it was her guilt, that was eating her up on the inside.

If God instructs you to do something, you will have the spirit to do it in humiliation. Never once did she say to me, when she gave me the stereo set that she purchased from Rent A Center some years ago, that she was paying me back, and if that was the case, I could have sworn the Lawyer gave her a check, and not a top of the line Kenwood system "Hello", "Can the Church say Yes and Amend".

This is why it is important for folk to read proverbs, because it teaches us not to argue with fools, and knowledge in knowing who the true living is God is. So she only ended up giving me a couple of month's worth, until I finally called her out on her foolishness, and told her I did not want it. I also said to her if it was a God thing she would have done it in the right manner, and not come up with all kinds of excuses, which I was already a custom too, see she wanted me to dance this dance with her, and trusting and believing that every month she was going to give me a hundred dollars, when in fact as soon as her money was deposited into her account she would be out on a binge, and no where to be found, until she returns broke and mad at the world. I felt like I was dealing with my X lover, whom I was with for ten years, and married too for four and a half years, until my light bulbs came on, Hmmm makes you wonder. She took from me, as well as He took from his Mother, and some other folks, but worst, **("you will understand it better by and by"),** be careful what you do, because sometimes your past will come back to bite you in the ass, what's done in the dark, will eventually come to the light.

Chapter Ten

At this point of my life; I started doing what ever I wanted to do because I just could not stand the fact of being in the house, and around my birth Mother who is, and still is in a dark place, because of all the drug abuse, I remember a time when I had some sort of medical issue going on, and did not no what it was, but all I know, is the fact that I was having a discomfort sensation when ever it came time for me too urinate, and I did not no what to do, and I did not even mention a word to the egg giver, because again she did not care, I "Thank you Jesus", because he saved me, and sent me to the doctors on my own, and I found out that I had caught a sexually transmitted disease though someone I was involved with, and that it was curable, and for ten days I had to take a antibiotic to clear up the infection, still I was lost, I had no one too talk to about it, and it hurt me to know that some unclean, selfish, and inconsiderate bastard would do such a thing to another, and I really could not pin point who did it, I was just trusting folk, and looking for love, because there was no love at 185 Walnut Ave, and no one ever taught me, or ever took the time to show me how to use a condom.

Eventually I was able to make some friends at the Boys and Girls club, because there were nights where we would go to parties and have a good time, and somebody please tell me what gives a sixteen year old the right to drink Sisco at such a young age. Well there it is, I was drinking yes at such a young age, I did not know what I was doing, but all I know is that I was having fun, and I did what I knew best to hide all the hurt and pain that I was felling inside. Still to this present day I'm trying to figure out how I made it home on a bicycle from Franklin Field projects, too Walnut Ave in Roxbury, After drinking four 40 oz of Old English, oh yes I remember that day like it was yesterday, and now I know it was God, and all I can say is "Thank you Jesus".

I remember coming home that day, and before I went into the house I stopped across the street at my friend Liz's house, who use to work with me at McDonalds' in the Lafayette Mall Downtown Boston. When I got there, Liz and some other people were already outside on the front steps, and when she ever looked into my eyes, she said "Korey, are you drunk?" I could not do anything but laugh, because I was tore up, from the floor up, eventually I went into the house and slept that mess off. Later on that night I was awakened by a car that blew its horn outside my bedroom window, and when I got up to look out the window I automatically new who it was.

It was this man who I met while I was working at Burger King that was on St. James St. inside the old Greyhound bus terminal, and how I met him was quite odd, I remember receiving a phone call one evening while I was working, and before I took the call I asked my supervisor who was it, and she said that the man said he was my Uncle. I startled because I knew right then and there it was not one of my

Uncles, because I never had a relationship with neither of them. The only things that I ever did with them, was to go and help them out with their Gardening, and sometimes go fishing and neither of those things interested me. The only reason why I would go with them to help them out was because of the fact that I made them pay me, and they did not do much work in the garden, but sit in the van and smoke their pipes and cigars, and drink cognac. When I took the phone call, I heard the voice of a man saying to me, "hello Korey", and I said, "What the hell", and "who is this?" trying to figure out how this man knew my name.

So eventually he gave me his number, and I called him back twenty minutes before my shift had ended, too see if we could meet up, because I was not going home until I found out who this mystery man was. Late that night we ended up meeting one another, and it just so happened that this man did not live too far from where I was living, and it was about a twenty minute walk from my house to his. When I got there we talked and I began to ask him some questions, as to why did he call my job and say that he was my Uncle, and what was his motive, and before I even got to his house, I had a clue to what was his motive was, and my mind was running rapid, and I was flattered in a way, but nervous and anxious in another, trying to figure out who this mystery man was. He told me that he had been watching me for a while and that he worked next door at the telephone company, and that Burger King was one of the places where he would go to have lunch. By this time I had put two and two together, he knew my name, because of my name tag.

It was around 12:30 am when I finally left his house to go home, and on the way home I was just in awe; because I did not know what to do, I had never been in relationship, and I did not know if this man was going to kill me, or rape me, I was scared, and nervous but happy at the same time.

I was feeling empty, and finally along comes someone that saw an interest in me, yes it was late, and it was a school night, but things did not matter much to me any more, and I did not care what my so –called Mother had to say, because she was already gone and lost in her own world, because of her drug addiction, sometimes she was home when I came home late, but she did not have much too say, why? Because she was already on cloud nine. Here I am at the age of sixteen, stuck, lost, broken, and lonely. With no sense of direction, no support no love just completely fucking empty inside, with no one to turn too, doing any and everything to make it on my own at such a young age. This man was nine years older than me, and at that time it did not really matter, because I got to know him for whom he was.

I spent most of my time at his house, and we did things like going to the movies etc... but he was the first to introduce me to the night life of going to the gay clubs, in and around the city of Boston. I remember one club that we went too, that was on Cambridge St., diagonally across from MGH called Sporter's, and when I ever walked up in that place to only see people that I knew from church, made me wonder. I can expose a lot of folks, but I will be nice, but what behooves me is that they try to act like heterosexuals, whenever they are around church folk, and what they don't seem to realize is that they are only fooling themselves, because everyone knows their situation.

What gets me; is the fact that some of them even dated women and had children knowing that they are gay, but instead they lived, and still live in such total darkness to cover up what they do not want others to know. They come to church with their toe nails painted in different colors to match the Choir robe, or whatever attire they may be wearing for that day. They sit up on the pulpit in wolfs clothing trying to tear down the walls of Jericho, when they cant even get right themselves, because they are such saints," A Saint sucking Dick with a sick Dick". Oh yes there are some men out there walking around living doubled lives, and carrying deadly diseases and not telling anyone, and infecting whom ever they can.

They don't seem to see anything they do wrong, "oh no", they shit don't' stink, meanwhile they have the drug dealers running in and out of the church, looking for them because they owe them money, and their Mama has to call other siblings in another state to send money to rescue them. My only thing with all of this is be who you are, and be real about it, God made you in his own likeness and image, and he created all of us different and unique in His own way, that's why we have African Americans, Hispanics, Caucasians, Orientals, . If God calls you to be a Minister or a Deacon, and you know that the Church does not accept your sexual orientation, who are you going to listen to? The voice of the Lord, or the Pastor telling you that you are not ready, and that you have to change your sexual orientation in order to serve the people of God. Again, "I say", **"He ho is without sin, please cast the first stone",** be who you are, and do it with dignity, and humiliation, and knowing that God is going to get all the glory. Who are they to judge, when God called me to become a Minister, I struggled with that because I did not know what to do, and "Yes", I went out on a limb seeking guidance from other clergy men, and got persecuted, **("You will understand it better by and by")**. It wasn't until he gave me my instruction, and said that you are going to be a Minister through writing, see God did not see fit for me too sit on any body's pulpit to minister too the same old stupid, and dumb folk who been sitting on pew number two for thirty eight years, and who still come too church, Sunday after Sunday in the same mess that they were in last Sunday, and the year before, the only thing that changes about them, is their clothing, and half of them can't even wear what they have, because of them being too Fat, or black & ugly, instead of dark & lovely, and no matter what they do to enhance the blackness, it makes what ever they are wearing clash, and that's why they come to church looking a hot and unsanctified mess, wearing bright orange lipstick, looking like the gorillas in the midst, or better yet, FUBU, (fat, ugly, black and uncomfortable), and they often like to carry on hell, and havoc during Choir rehearsals, or in any auxiliary that they are a member off, and give the president or the musician their ass to kiss, and Deacons, and Deaconesses who look like kin folk to those flying Monkey's, from the movie, The Wiz, "BRING ME MY MONKEY'S", "PEW WEE" ("Kill the visual Jesus", "Kill the visual"). That's why this book is published with I Universe, because God wanted me too touch the Universe, instead of those dead weight Sunday after Sunday worshipers, and God knew all the hell I would have gone through, to proclaim what he has called me to be, and that is why this book is titled **"I'm Not Going Mad, I'm Just Coming Into Myself"**. I am who I am, and if you have a problem with that, take it up with the Father in Heaven and see if he gives a Rats Ass, about what any of you all have to say. He who has begun a new work in me shall complete it until the day of Jesus Christ, like the song writer Daryl Coley said, he is sovereign, God can do whatever he wants too do, when he wants too, and who am I to question his wisdom, I am nothing, he is God all by himself and he does not need anybody's help, think about it, and then start shouting. This is why many of us miss our blessings, because we are so quick to judge and tear down one another, and many are filled with jealousy and envy, and will do whatever to get what some else has, this is also called living beyond your means, if you cant afford it, give it back, don't worry about what others may have to say, because they are struggling too, but they don't want you to know it. If you don't have it, it is because it is not your season to have it, and you don't know all the hell that person had to go through in order to receive what God has given them. God gives us things accordingly, and there are times when he challenges us to seek what we long for; but in the right spirit, a lot of you do not know what true faith is, ask me, and I will tell you. We are supposed to rejoice when we see some one being blessed, not get upset, and try to live beyond our means to get what they have. God sends Angels in many different forms, and half of you all miss them, because your heart is hardened. The working of the Holy Spirit does not require authorization for any Minister to go to seminary school, Jesus did not go to Gordon Conwell, and neither did Luke, John, Mathew, Paul or Peter. None of them received a master's degree. Instead they received the Master's instructions, which are greater and more powerful than a piece of paper that states; you have completed the necessary requirements in Urban Ministries.

This is why the pulpits are over crowded with robotically, and mechanically ordained, and trained Ministers, because they are lost in what it really means to be called to be a Minister, all they do is sit up on the pulpit and collect dust, and wait for instructions to either bring forth the word, or read a scripture, or call to worship, better yet, responsive reading, and some are being used to sing because of the gift that they have to sing, because the leader of the church don't have the anointed voice to sing, and needs someone to pump up the congregation. You would think that they were servants for the Pastor of the church, and the only time some of them received the chance to speak, is when the Sheppard is either away on vacation or ministering out of town, and what puts the icing on the cake, is the fact that some of them get paid to preach. I am a living witness to that, because there were several occasions' where I had to wait in the car while my significant other waited for one of the Deacons, or Trustees to hand him his check, I'm so glad to know that the God I serve is cashing checks on a daily basis, because you never know, where your next financial blessing is going to come from.

What behooves me is that you have some church folk who have been in the church for years, and don't have a clue to what is going on behind closed doors, why? Because the Pastors only tell you what they want you to know at these annual church meetings, because they don't want the members to know the mistakes, and the mess they have created, did they forget that they are not perfect themselves?, did they not realize that God allowed these mistakes to happen to see if they are humbled enough to stand in humiliation, in front of the church body?, and reconcile what they have done wrong, what is the sense of having a church covenant if you are not going to lead by example, and what ever happened to God's covenant? Everyone is not called to pastor a Church, like God told Peter to write 1st & 2nd Peter, he told me to write 1st & 2nd J'Korey Mills. Further more; who called them too be Dr. Bishops, Reverends, and Fathers. I believe God called us to be Ministers, prophets and Apostles, where did all of these man made titles come from?, next thing you know they are going to have Pope's and Cardinals in the Baptist churches, and there is only one Father, and He is in heaven, and I am not about to walk up in no church, and began to call God's chosen, "Father Richie", because there is only one way to the father and that's is through our Savior Jesus! What really behooves me is their traditional ways of serving God, where is it written that Deacons and Deaconesses are supposed to wear white on first Sundays in the spring and summer seasons, and Black Suits in the winter. Who told them that we are supposed to only have communion on every first Sunday of the month, I believe that the scripture says for us too take as often as you can, in remembrance of me, so that means that we can take part of the last supper on any given day, and it does not have to be in church, you could be at home in your car or even at work, there is no law saying that we are not allowed to commune, or anoint yourselves, and that we have to be a licensed or an ordained, and robotically trained Minster. A lot of these pastors are just only preaching church, instead of teaching Christ, it does not matter what you wear too Church or how you look, what really matters is that you come to serve Jehovah, He knows your heart, and he does not measure our hearts by what we wear, or what we look like. Another thing that is disturbing; that I don't think some of these pastors are aware of, is that when the Holy spirit is coming forth, and moving in a rapid speed, often times I see Pastors get up and signal the musician to slow the music down so that they can get a word in, don't they realize that they are playing with God when they interrupt the spirit coming forth, and that is not their time too Minister, and what they need to do is sit down and be still, and let God have his way, sometimes it is not meant for them to always minister a word, because when God shows up in spirit, the word has already come forth.

Eventually I was fired from Burger King and I had obtained another job working again at another MacDonald's, and was discharge from there as well, for the fact of stealing money out of the register, I did any and everything to survive. Ever since my friend introduced me to the clubs, that's where you would have found me on a Saturday night, by then I was now exploring and seeking more, and I started sleeping with other men not knowing what they were all about, again trying too find love, and to fulfill the void that was in my life.

There was a time when I was out so late, and the bus service had stopped running and I had to take a cab home, and knowing that I did not have any money to pay for the cab, I ended up giving the cab driver my long black goose down coat that had fur around the collar for collateral, because he was going to try to kill me for not having the money to pay him. I even Started Church hoping all because there was division that came upon the church that I was attending, the Junior and Kelly Choir #2 lost their musician all because of drama with the Deacons, there were Sundays where we would be in line to process in, and often times we had to come in singing without music , because we did not know if our musician was going to show up, all because of the mess and the drama that was going on, and what mad it so obvious, is because of the fact that something transpired at one of our rehearsals with him, and the Deacons. Sis Phillyaw, Sis. Searcy (rest in peace) had to be the bad news bears to all of us in the Jr. Choir, and Shortly after; we lost our associate Pastor who could preach a powerful sermon (Rest in Peace Rev. Gerald) all because of that mean and surly Pastor and founder of the Church.

From this point on everyone started fading away, and going to join other churches, the Moore Family ended up moving back to Alabama.

I started to wonder off going to other churches as well, I did not know what was going on, and I did not know how to handle what was happening, all I know is that things just went completely pandemonium. After struggling going to find a Church were I would feel most comfortable, I ended up going to one of the Local Churches in Mattapan. Even that was a nightmare because when it came time for me to join one of the choirs, I felt like I did not belong, because when the choir President ask the members to vote me in, no one responded, it took her two times before anyone had responded, I thank God for this one particular women who served as a trustee and was the director of the Mass Choir, because she was there to witness it all. In April of 2010 I participated in the reunion and trust and believe I was hesitant in doing so because of the treatment I received when I joined years ago. It was the former president, and the grace of God who inspired me into going, because the spirit of the Lord told me that I had nothing to fear, but fear itself, and I went and had fun in the name of Jesus, because I was over what had happened in the past and the fact that these people could no longer look down on me, neither judge me because I am a sinner saved by grace and half of them got some shit with them too.

G.G was special to me; because I did not have any friends, and neither did I have family, and everyone talked about me, and ridiculed me because I had a problem, yes a major one at that, I use to take money out of peoples pocket books in order to provide for myself, no one new my pain, and what I had to go through, and still too this day I walk alone, with only God on my side **("you will understand it better by and by")**. Does anyone know what it feels like to go to Church Sunday after Sunday being so young, lost and broken, and the fact of being the only child, and I would not have been the only child, but because my egg donor aborting her other three children before I was conceived, left me no choice, "further more", watching other families come and go in a happy spirit, and you on the other side of the picture wishing that were you? But yet and still, I went home Sunday after Sunday with nothing to eat in the house and no one to talk too, and no one to love me. These people did not know the pain that I had to bare, and what makes matters worst is that I had a cousin that attended the Church as well, and let the truth be known, he is not really related to us, and that he is one those people, who is just a close friend of the family, and he knew the issues I had in and around the Church, because of the fact that Church folk talked about me as if I was a piece of scum on the streets. This man talked about me like a dog to my family, ("bow, wow, wow, yippy yo, yippy yea) and everyone knew what was going on, and never once did he show compassion, and offer too take the time to sit down and talk with me to see what was going on. I did not receive much of any support from the Pastor as well, and every time I did something wrong I was sat down from the choir, and never did he seek to counsel me, but like most Pastors, who would rather not deal with the issues and carry on like nothing ever happened. I believe the bible teaches us to counsel the ungodly, so if you see some one doing something wrong you are supposed to talk with them, and encourage them of what they are doing wrong, not pass judgment, "What would Jesus Do!". As I look back and realize and see that churches have a way of punishing people for their wrong doings, again I say who are they to take charge in disciplining another human for there sinful ways. I ask myself; is this of God? Is this how we are supposed to treat one another in a Godly way? It would have been better if they just would have said; go back into the world, I could have accepted that a lot better, because sitting me down did not resolve my issue, it just made things more and more complicated, "Oh, yes", and don't dare have a baby out of wed-loc, they would sit you down for that too, it's like them running their own district courts inside the church, and the deacon board serves as jurors.

In the midst of all of it, I stood in complete humiliation and held my head high and continued on going to the church because there was no where else for me to go, the bridge had collapsed. There was one Lady who though her stuff did not stank, when everyone knew she was one of the biggest boosters in and around the city of Boston, yes I will admit I did something I should not have had done, "yes", I did steal her checks and went food shopping and bought me three hundred dollars worth of food, and "yes", she found out what I had did to her, and pressed charges against me, "yes", she made it known; especially at Church what I did.

"Oh yes", she showed her ass in the court room, and still to this day she calls me all kinds of nasty names over something that happened over thirteen years ago, and her favorite line is hold your pocket book, and she loves reminding me that I am a faggot. What she does not seem to realize that if she would take some time to look at herself deeply she will see some fault in herself as well. The scary part is that she is in Church every Sunday sitting on the front pew, and what she needs to realize is that God has a way of turning tables, and sometimes he uses us to turn the tables on others, "vengeance is mine said the Lord". Oh she wanted to prosecute me, oh yes she wanted me to go to jail, but then again, No weapon formed against me shall ever prosper, instead I was put on probation and had to pay her back the money through the court, and the bible tells us that we are not supposed to seek justice on one another, and that we are supposed to be doers and hearers of the word of God.

Instead of better, things turned for the ultimate worst, I was gone, and completely lost, I was taking from any and everybody, even some family members, I was sending all kinds of signs, but nobody was listening and taking heed to what was going on, I was a thief, and no one trusted me, and I was doing what I knew how to do in order to survive in a drug abused home, I remember coming home one evening from the Boy's and Girls club, and when I walked in the door, my egg donor who was looking like she just had come of cloud nine, said to me that my God Mother wanted to see me, and I asked her for what? And right then and there she got silent and skirted around the question and insists that I go over to her house. Meanwhile; here I am nervous, wondering what the hell she wanted me for, so I turned around and headed back out the door to my God Mother house who lived in walking distance. When I got their and walked through the door, I had already knew that something was not right, because I felt it in my spirit, when my God Mother sat me down with her daughter at the kitchen table, and began to ask me if I had taken her daughters gold bracelet, I was immediately heart broken, because I knew deep down in my heart that I did not take her jewelry, and when I told them that I didn't take it, they acted as though, as if they did not believe me, and that hurt me even more so, on top of everything else that I was dealing with. The two of them interrogated me in such a way that I just wanted to commit suicide, because finally here I am telling the truth and no one wants to believe me, because of my history of stealing and lying, but did they ever stop to think that it could have been one of the crack heads that was living in their house, who also participated in the crack sessions with my egg donor, "oh yes", how do I know? I was not set up, and "yes" I have dealt with it all these years, and took the blame for something I really in all honesty know, I did not do, and still to this present day I go around them with my head held high, and with a smile on my face, knowing that I was once persecuted by them, and them not knowing how I really feel about them on the inside, "oh", but they running scared, because they know that I am writing this book, and now they are wondering, if I have to say anything bad about them. The only thing that I have ever taken from My want to be so-called Godmother, was her youngest daughters suede shirt, and the reason being is because of the fact that I had always admired the way she dressed and the fact that I really did not have anything descent or new clothes to wear. I had to make do with what little bit of clothing I had, and her daughter did get her shirt back because my egg donor found it, and set me up one day and brought me to Her house, and pulled the shirt out of her bag in front of my 1st Cousin who calls herself my Godmother, and her daughter, "WOW', a mess, but still I stood in humiliation through all of that too, don't get me wrong, my want to be Godmother has a heart, but also some fucked up ways, as if she is better than you, because when I read to her my prologue, the first thing that came out of her mouth was, "You wrote that", and she said it in a way as if I was stupid, as if I didn't know how to read, think or write, and what behooves me is that she now walks around like she is so holy than thou all because she gave her life back too Christ a few years ago, and what she don't seem to realize that she is still nothing but a baby Christian, and like pastor Hurt once said, we have Baby and Mature Christians, and the scary part is that she is a Sunday school teacher, and sometimes folk really need to examine themselves before they take upon a gift that they are not capable to do.

Through it all; I thank God for G.G, because she stood by me like a Mother, and it is so true what the scripture says in Mark Chapter 3:35 Whoever does God's will is my Brother, Sister and Mother. This women invited me into her home and not one time did I ever take anything from her, she fed me, and took care of me, and she new deep down what I was dealing with because I trusted her enough to open up and talked to her, its funny because I think back at the times how I use to wait for her to come out of the trustees room and often times I would knock to let her know I was waiting for her.

People use to say negative things about me to her; they could not understand how she could be around me for all the things I did in the Church, but not once did she listen to them, she kept loving me to the point where I became apart of her family and was invited to spend the holidays with them as well. Our relationship is broken right now, but I pray that God will repair it, and yes I did something devastating and you will understand it better, by and by. She was not the only one that was there for me; there was another women who had a compassion for children, and all I can say is thank you Jesus for Sis Christine Calloway (Rest In Peace), because she took me in as well, and often times I would go and spend the weekend with her, with her and her Daughter, and I can truly say that this women new and saw for herself what was going on in my home, for the simple fact that she wanted too meet my egg donor, and wanted to make sure that it was ok for me to spend the weekend with her. Sometimes Nola who also sung in the same choir with me, would be there too, and Sis. Calloway would cook, and believe you me we ate, until our soul was content, and she loved making egg custard pie, Like the song writer once said, may the works I've done, speak for me, when I am resting in my grave, Lord don't let my living be in vain, my the life I live speak for me.

Chapter Eleven

Spring of 1991 we ended up moving to Braintree Ma, all because my so-called Egg Donor liked the apartments better, and the fact that one of her friends who she use too get high with lived in the complex, with her three kids, and her youngest daughters father, who is from New York, and a hot mess himself.

I remember the day we had moved from 185 Walnut Avenue in Roxbury Ma, and my Egg Donor ended up leaving a lot of stuff, because she could not find no one to help her move, and I was no where around to help her, and I don't even recall packing, because I was so distant from her, and I was not really sure of what I wanted to do. That night I had to go and sing with my Choir and when we finished singing, I asked someone to give me a ride to the train station, and there I was, on the Red Line heading to Braintree ma, it did not dawn on me that she left a lot of things behind until I got there and saw it for myself.

The only things she made sure she brought with her was her bed, and TV and clothes, and I was glad that she took into consideration in moving my clothes, and my little Black and white TV that I had won selling the most candy when I was six. "Yes"; that TV has come along way, "Thank you Jesus!!!" And as time went on she began to rent stuff from Rent a Center and using the money she would receive from the department of public welfare to pay for it, "a mess". I had no bedroom furniture, so I had to sleep on the floor for a while, and I had some milk crates that were brought over from the old apartment, and I used them to build a shelving unit to put my clothes in. It was not until my family members, who came to pick us up to go out to Bridgewater Ma, to Visit some kin folk. When they came in to see the apartment and my Aunt saw that I did not have a bed, that's when she told me that she had an extra full size brand new box spring and mattress, and that I could have it, and truly I thank God for her that day.

I must admit; that I thought moving to Braintree was a great idea, it was time for a change, a big change, finally we were gone from the drug infested crime fighting inner city. The complex we moved into was far better than any of the apartments we lived in. It was like paradise, we had a dish washer, and a front balcony, chandelier lighting in the dinning room that was on a dimmer switch, a big pool that was located at the front entrance of the complex, with a full indoor recreational area.

The size of my bedroom was big and spacious, and the view from my window over looked the parking lot that was on the side of the building, and beyond the parking lot was a grassy, and swampy looking area, and just beyond all of that was a train track. Every now and then you would see the old looking freight trains move. Other than that the trains would just sit there, day after day, what they used them for? I do not know, and not once did I inquire. It was just like living in the country, with a peace of mind, no gun shots, no fear of being robbed or beaten when walking home at night, it was none of that, it was like God saying Peace be Still!, and the only disadvantage was getting too and from the store, because walking to the nearest store could take you almost and hour. Once again; it was hard making friends, but I did, thanks to my Best friend Laverne's ex-boyfriend, who lived in the building across from me. I started hanging out with him and his friends for a while, until he turned against me. It was also a new beginning for me, because I was now going to attend public school for the first time in nine years, I was so glad to know that I did not have to go back to Edna Stein Academy, ("Thank you Jesus"), because that school was like a living hell. I spent the summer hanging out meeting new people until September of 1991 when school had begun. I remember walking to the bus stop which was located at the front of the Complex, and while I was standing there I was feeling a little unease, because of the fact that I could feel the negative vibes coming from some of what I would call, want to be African American Thuggish Caucasian boy's, who hung out with me, and who I was introduced too, by my best friends ex-boyfriend, who eventually turned on me, and who also told them some negative stuff about me, because from that point on, I was their target.

What behooves me is that C was much older than these boys, and I often wondered why would somebody who is out of high school would belittle themselves and hang out with punks. C new I was gay from the beginning, because he use to talk to my best friend, and one day while I was walking through Washington Park, I ran into Laverne, and she was with him. That's how I meet and knew who he was.

I had never seen him before, up until this point, and when I met him for the very the first time, he kind of starred me, and looked me up and down as if he thought I was checking him out.

"Oh yes", I was checking him out, and yes he was cute, but behind it all was cheap foundation that you would have purchased from a thrift store. His attitude sucked, and I felt it, but little did he know, I was not interested in him at all, but I could feel and sense that he was intimated by me, like most straight acting guys are, and that's why I did not fit in to his click. I was called all kinds of names while I was standing there at the bus stop, and what made matters even worst, is that I had to deal with the negativity from his sister, and her friends as too.

I thought moving so far out and away from the city was supposed to be a peace of mind, but my summer was like living in hell, and to know that I had to go to school everyday with these cats, was going to be even more eventful. In the midst of all of this, I held my head up and pressed on.

I just started looking at the fact that I did not have to go back to an alternative program, and what a challenge is was going to be for me to attend classes in a public school setting.

Here I am again; alone and lost, trying to find my way through a school that was the size of Holy Cross College in Worcester Ma, I was glad to know that none of those haters who lived in my neighborhood was in any of my classes. I thank God because I was able to make one friend on my own, who was in the same Biology class as me, and who was also in the same study block, and he happened to live on the Braintree, and Holbrook line.

Sometimes I would wait until his bus would arrive before entering the school and going to my locker, he also introduced me to his girlfriend Laurie, and from that point on they were the only two I hung out with. Laurie attended a Catholic Church, and I remember going to church with her and V one Sunday, and I tell you it was a first for me, because I had never been in a Catholic Church for any type of service, and for me to be brought up in a Baptist Church was far different from what went on in this particular Church, and the fact of not knowing the difference between the two religions.

I did not get much out of what was going on, because I was too busy trying to keep up with all the hail Mary's, and the tradition that they were a custom too, and it was not working, I felt embarrassed, because I was in such delay in what they were doing, and could not keep up.

"Ok"; where was the choir, and the sermon, and most of all the Holy Ghost, it was a dead Church, I felt like shouting John, "Hold My Mule", but I must say I was glad to be in the house of the Lord one more time. It was hard for me to attend church now, because we lived so far out, and if, and when I did have the chance to go to my home church, I use to take the MBTA, and sometimes GG would bring me home, and I was grateful, that this women went the extra mile to do so.

As time continued on, I eventually made some more friends at BHS, and my relationship with V and his girlfriend eventually faded, and I started hanging out with theses two girls R & I, who lived around the corner from me outside of the complex. Until one day after school I went to go hang out with them, and while we were outside, doing nothing but talking, and hanging out I asked one of the kids if I could use his bike to go home and check on the house, and to see if my egg donor was there.

As I walked outside of my building to go and return the bike that I had borrowed, I was stopped by the Braintree Police, and one of the officers got out of the cruiser, and questioned me as too who's bike it was that I had, and when I told them, immediately they did not seem to believe what I was saying, and said to me that it was reported stolen. Right then and there they arrested me and read me my Miranda rights. I often wonder if I was white would they have arrested me, because none of the kids that I hung around with was neither black, it sadden me, because I did not see anything I did wrong, but through it all God was in the midst.

When I arrived at the police station they booked me, and allowed me to make one or two phone calls, and after several attempts of trying to reach my egg donor, she finally came to get me out of that hell hole. I was not only charged with larceny, but rape as well, and how dare those white girls lie on me, and say such things, when in fact I had never ever once tried to have sexual contact with them, and neither did I have a interest in either of them, and for the most part, pussy is not my thing, in fact I was looking for the same thing they was looking for, a piece of dick, like I tell folk today, I am strictly dickly. What behooves me is that you have women who might have an interest in you, tell you, that you have not had the right pussy, and someone please tell me, what is the right kind of pussy.

I thank God for the judge who through the case out, because he saw it for himself, that it was a Black & White issue, racism that is, and this was not the first incident that had taken place between me and the Braintree Police Department, I had to testify against another kid who use to bully me at school, and for him doing so much crime they was looking for him, and I had to talk to the detectives, and make unnecessary court appearances as a witness. It would have been better, if we had just stayed, in what I call the ghetto, why my egg donor up and decided to move to a town that was filled with such racism and hatred has me flabbergasted. From that point, I did not want to live there anymore, and neither did I want to go back to BHS. I did continue to go to school, and started skipping classes, and wondering the corridors, and often times I would find myself in the guidance counselor's area to avoid the noise.

I met this woman by the name of Doreen, who was a special education advisor, who saw that I was lost, and that being in such a big School, without any help of peers and teachers was a bit much for me, and it was. Miss Doreen then spoke with a lady by the name of Dr. Zimmerman who was the head of special Ed, who I meet once before school started, when my egg Donor was enrolling me into school.

Who then scheduled a meeting with me and my so-called Mother to make arrangements for me to go into another alternative program, and which I did, I can't think of the name of the school they sent me too, and it was not for long, because eventually they kicked me out, because of my disruptive behavior. In the midst of all of what was going on, I was still lacking what I needed at home from a Mother, things did change with her, they went for the ultimate worst, to the point where I had to file a 51A on myself, because it was days, and nights that my so-called Mother did not come home, and I was tired of coming home to a empty home and refrigerator, that barely had any food in it. I could not call on any family members, because they were all caught up in their own shit, and nobody wanted me around, because of the fact that I have a mouth, and a temper, and at the time I was stealing, and most of all, I am gay, no one in my family liked or accepted the fact that I am gay, and again, I "say" "I am, who I am, said Sam I am, who would not eat green eggs and ham". I am not going to live my life to please others, and God made me who I am, and nobody has too deal with who I am, but God, and who are they too judge. When I met with the social worker out of the Weymouth Ma, office, he put me into a respite home for a couple of nights until he could find me another place to go, and also while he tried to locate my egg donor. Meanwhile; my social worker could not locate her anywhere, and eventually I transferred from respite, into a semi group home, and after being there for a while my worker found and located my egg donor. Trying to schedule a meeting with her was impossible, because she made up excuses as to why she did not want to meet, I did in fact talk to her on the phone and was able to contract with the group home, and the social worker to go and see her. It was a Saturday when I got the chance to go see her only in Boston where she was at my cousin's house on Tremont St. in the South End, who also had a problem with using drugs. I remember that day very well, because I ended up coming back to the group home drunk, why because she had bought me liquor to drink. When I returned to the group home, they knew I was drunk because I started acting out in such disruptive behavior, and you could also smell the alcohol on my breath. I was hurt, and blinded, to why, and when, was all of this going to stop, I just wanted to be in a normal home, and shortly thereafter, I was discharged from this group home, because I ended up destroying the place (Another Madea), then my Case Manager ended up taking me too this foster home out on the cape in Orleans Ma, in the meanwhile; my Social Worker placed my name on the placement list at the Fall River diagnostic assessment center in Fall River Ma,. I had to go into foster care until a placement had become available, here I am, in no mans land, straight up country. My Worker had placed me with this couple who were in their late seventies, and all I know is that they looked old Bain, and crippled, they had two dogs, and there was another guy that stayed there, and his name was Paul, he also shared the same room with me in the attic, and come to find out, he was a recovering alcoholic who needed a place to stay. This house was absolutely beautiful, and by the looks of the inside and out you knew that theses couples had some Benjamin's, in fact we ate out almost every other night.

I enjoyed being there because it was peaceful and quiet, until the day, the day when the foster father lured me into him and his wife's bedroom, where there were only two twin beds, and that was a first for me to see, because I thought that married couples shared the same bed, and that's when he began to try to molest me, and immediately I ran out of the room, and went outside to smoke a cigarette in a state of shock, not knowing which way to go, and who the hell to turn too. I did not trust anyone, nor did I tell anyone, not even my social worker who did not make home in time enough to have dinner with his wife, because he had to come get me in a hurry, because I was so upset of the fact, of what just happened, and I began to destroy their house. I felt bad for the foster mother because she had no clue as to what her husband had done; all I remember is hearing her saying to my worker is that I had to go. Thank you Jesus, and was I ever glad to go; when my social worker came to get me late that evening, he told me that just upon him leaving the office he received a phone call from the Fall River Diagnostic Assessment center that a bed had become available (He's an On Time God, Yes He Is). While in route from Orleans Ma, to Fall River Ma, my worker explained to me that the place where I was going was a ninety day assessment center, and that it was a non smoking program, "what the hell". In the meanwhile here I am trying to smoke four packs of cigarettes at one time just to get rid of them, I even asked my case worker if he could hold on to them until I got out,(Laugh out Loud) he told me no, but not in a mean way. Nine O'clock that evening we finally arrived and my Social worker stayed with me through out the intake interview, and I ended up sharing a room with this kid whose feet smelled like A Shitting Ass Mess, and whom I did not get along with very well because we had nothing in common, and the fact that he was a dirty and unclean individual, and his underwear had shit stains in them, and he would leave them any and everywhere in the room.

The reasoning for me going into this program was the fact that they were going to assess me, to see where I was at academically and too see what kind of services I needed, because I did not, and I refused to go back home to live with the egg donor. Some individuals either moved on to other group homes, or foster homes, but in my case, because I was seventeen at the time they prepared me to go into an independent living program. While I was at the Assessment center I managed to speak with my egg donor, who eventually came to see me with my Aunt, who took me out to eat, and to the mall, I must say it was nice to see her, and the fact that the visit went well, but still there were underlying issues that have not been resolved.

My social worker told me prior, that my egg donor checked herself into a drug rehab program, and that she did not want me to know, and that explains why she was missing for so long. The assessment center was kind of like The Home for little Wanderers, except for the fact, that we were on a one floor unit on the very top floor of the Fall River YMCA, and all the doors were locked, and if someone decided to run away the doors would have alarmed, and there were locked screens all around the windows, and I guess they had to secure the windows to prevent any of them fools from opening, and jumping their crazy asses out the window (How Low Can You Go). Eventually I was transferred into my own room for the simple fact that I could not stand the fact of having a room mate any more, and also because my roommate use to sneak cigarettes into the unit whenever he would returned from a family visit, and one night we got caught smoking in the room, and staff then had to shut the unit down and do a room search, not only did they search our room they searched everyone else's, and believe you me, they were all pissed because the room search took place late that night, just before the third shift had started.

Like most residential programs, I did have an advocate, and his name was Johnathan and at first I gave him a hard time because I had issues with being in around men, I did not feel comfortable because of what I had already been through, but to know that he was gay, and it was obvious, it made me put down my guard a little bit towards him, because finally there was someone I could talk too, and relate too.

I enjoyed being in my own room, because I enjoyed the pleasure of listening to my gospel music and having church at my own leisure. Sometimes I would even get a crowed at my door, and staff and some residents joined in with me singing, as I stood there directing the walls to the remix of former Rap Artist Mc Hammer, singing Pass Me Not O Gentle Savior. Oh yes I had them having church, and what's interesting is that staff would bring me more gospel music to listen too, and trust and believe, it brought me through a lot, (When the praises go up, the blessings will come down). There was one staff by the name of Francis, who had her own motto, and that was "don't mess with Francis, she don't take no chances", she was one of the main ones who supplied me with various gospel music. Now as I look back and see, that serving the Lord has paid off, because I look at where I am today in life, and I can truly say that in the midst of whatever was going on, and it did not matter where I was, and I did not care who was offended about me serving my God, I still gave God, Extravagant Praise. To see the angels that he sent to surround me, and comfort me and protect me, makes me happy to know that he was there all the time, because there were many of nights I cried, because of the pain I had to go through of not having a normal life, and the cards that were being dealt, and just excepting what ever came my way.

Chapter Twelve

When my ninety days had finally ended, I moved on to another program, but this time it was an Independent Program located in Brockton Ma. The name of this program was called The Growing Minds Resource Institute, and in it, were two programs in one, but in different locations. I could have moved back home, but I decided that I did not want too, and I only had one more year to go before I had turned eighteen years of age to sign myself out of DSS custody.

The purpose of this program was for me too mainstream into my own apartment, and as well as obtaining a job and being responsible for paying my bills, (life skills) this was one of the most intense programs that I have ever been in, because we had to be out the house by eight am looking for work or either enrolled in school. I was blessed because I had resumed back into going to a special needs school that was located in Whitman Ma, called the North River Collaborative, even this was new for me, because I was out of school ever since the day I was put into a respite home.

I was only allowed to contract to go home on the weekends, and that's if I wanted too, because by this time I and my want to be Mother did not see eye to eye, why?

Because of her trying too tell me what to do, and trying to gain control over me and my thoughts. By this time I had lost total respect for her, why? Because she did not have any respect for herself, and neither did she have any respect for me as her child. We always argued, even still too this present day, why because she can't see herself for what it really is. I will not dare listen to her trying to chastise me and correct me and tell me how to live my life when she did not show a good enough example, especially too her nieces and nephews who she was getting high with. When my eighteenth birthday came, I ended up signing myself out of the independent living program and moving back home with my egg donor, why because I still was hoping and praying that she would get better, and for a minute she was on the right track, because while me being in DSS custody she went back to school to become a Certified nurses assistant, and I was happy for her, and I did attend her graduation, and she did end up finding work in her field.

There was one night while I was asleep and she came home with this guy, and hours latter I was awakened by this man that looked like one of those trolls that people would carry to bingo for luck. This man asked me if I had knew where she was, and I told him that I did not know, and all he kept saying is that she has my car, and from that point on, I knew she was back out there using again.

This man was incoherent himself, to the point where he got on my last nerve and I told him that she was across the street, just to get him the hell out so that I could go back to sleep.

Still at times there was no food in the house and she continued to meet these men who would often times buy food for me and her, and it really did not matter much to me anymore, because while I was at the independent living program I managed to get a job working at the Brockton Boy's and Girl's Club, and I commuted from Braintree to Brockton everyday, and eventually that job had ended , but before I even started working there as a staff member, I did some volunteer work with this women by the name of Denise Baker Bradley, whom I was introduced too by my advocate at the Growing minds resource institute.

Eventually I met this Caucasian male who is gay; through someone I associated myself with in the complex. He was not all that, but I settled for whatever, and he was a lot older than me, and the reason of me being with him was the fact that I wanted, and needed someone to show me, and give me love and affection. Eventually I moved out of her apartment to go and live with him in Weymouth Ma, and shortly after me moving in with him, the Land Lord told me and him that I had to leave, because apparently when I left the house, I forgot to shut off the coffee pot that almost set the entire house on fire. This man was in love with me, because he ended up moving back with me into the hell hole, with the permission of my so-called Mother.

Its was not even a good month after moving back inn with her, that we ended up having to move quick fast, and in a hurry, because she use to harass him in the late midnight hours while I was at work about money, and yes he did pay her rent for staying there, but she acted like she was not getting enough, and she just wanted more so that she could continue to get high. He had a good job as a store manager, and in fact he got me a job within the company. I worked the eleven to seven shifts at the Christy's Market in Weymouth landing, and he was the store manager of the Christy's market in Randolph Ma, and the store I worked at was in walking distance from the apartment complex. When I met this man, and after dating him for a couple of days, he told me something that was devastating to hear, and what he told me was that he was HIV positive, and when he told me that, it sort of blew my mind, because I did not know what HIV was. All I knew that is was a disease that killed people, and in fact I know a few people who have died from it. Immediately after him disclosing to me his situation, I got tested myself, and found out that I was positive too, it devastated me to hear what I herd come out of the Doctors mouth, because all I kept thinking about was the fact that I did not have much time too live, and why me? When I look back over my life, and I began to think things over, I realize that it was not him that infected me. It was someone else who gave me this deadly disease, someone whom I was once involved with, when I was around the age of fifteen-sixteen years old. I know the person who did this to me, and they are now dead and gone. Thank You Jesus! For revealing the truth of who infected me, because for the longest I blamed it on the guy who was honest enough to tell me his situation from the beginning and the person who infected me was a former member of the Kelly Choir #2. Eventually we ended up moving to Randolph, where I ended up going back to High School, and In 1994 I ended up graduating from the Randolph Jr. Sr. High School, with the help and support of my significant other, who gave me a wonderful graduation party, as well as a twenty first birthday party where my best friend Laverne showed up, and I thank those who supported me on my graduation day, My Egg Donor of course, who looks like death walking, and its amazing what these drugs can do to a person, and how it makes them look on the inside as well as the outside, and most of all my God Mother, who gave me a hundred dollars to go and buy a new outfit for that day. It was a tough assignment going back to School, because I had too push myself through it all, just to obtain my high school diploma, knowing that I was HIV positive, and scared in not knowing how much time I had left to live here on earth. Still to this very day, I do not receive support from anyone but a chosen few, and thank God for them.

While we were living in Randolph, I did have an affair with another man who I was introduced too by my cousin who lived around the corner from me, and later on I found out that he was a crack head, how? Because he would always ask me for money, and would also ask me to drop him off in drug infested neighborhoods. When I confronted her, and asked her about it, she told me that she thought he had stopped using drugs, and apologized to me for it, not only was he a crack head, but he was also HIV positive, and for some odd reason, this man was infatuated with me, because every time I would go to visit my cousin, who lived on Cheney St, he would come by and ring her bell, and she would go to the window in my defense and tell Him to stop ringing her bell and that I was not coming outside. This man knew whenever I was there, because of the fact that he knew what kind of car I drove, and he would always see my car parked outside, this man lived on Maple St. which was a block away from my cousins house, my cousin yelled at me, when she ever found out that we knew each other, and she confirmed, what I had already had discovered about him, and she told me to stay away from him, and I did, and I thank God for my cousin because she protected me from danger seen and unseen, and What's scary about this, is that this guy use too date my x- spouse, who I was once married too, **(You will understand it better by and by)**, she never liked him, for the simple fact that he tried to hit on her man, and because he was no good. "Yes", this man, I must say, had a drop dead gorgeous looking body at the time, but again that goes too show you that everything that glitters, and looks good, is not gold. Again, I say, too many folk walking around here with sick dicks, and sick pussy's, and I'm here to tell you, get it checked, before you inject, as well as drug screening and criminal back ground check.

April 5 1995; I should have been dead and sleeping in my grave, but because of the grace of God, he kept me, and my significant other. When we were struck, and broad sided by another vehicle, which made our car skid, and flip upside down in front of a church member's house, that I use to attend church with. My significant other did not believe in

God, but I can truly say that he supported me at church when ever it came time for Choir Anniversaries, and not one time did he ever discourage me from going. It was not until I met him, when I started back going to the local church where I suffered much persecution in Mattapan Ma, and when I returned, I became a member of the Mass Choir, who had the same musician, as the past and former choirs I use to sing in, and not long after I had joined the choir, there was mess going on with the musician and the pastor of that church, and again we lost a powerful musician. G.G who was the director, and her Mother who was the Choir President, were left trying to keep the choir together with the help of other musicians, In the midst of our struggles the choir lost a few members, but through it all we were still able to give God the highest praise, we continued on with traveling with our Pastor too other states to visit other Churches, this was the first time that I have ever gone out of state to sing, and I must say, I did enjoy the trip to Baltimore Maryland, and what happened on that trip between me and the musician at the time, still remains a mystery, and all I can say is "Lord Have Mercy",. There were others in the choir, that I knew who were Gay, or bisexual, because of the fact that I had a semi relationship with them prior, and during my relationship with my significant other, who bored the hell out of me, to the point where I started seeking elsewhere to fulfill the void ("Don't hate the player, hate the game, and only trust God").

I knew a lot of these folk were not stupid, and knew what was going on with me, because of the fact that I did not hide who I was, and I was proud to bring my significant other to church, and did not give a damn about what those ignorant ass church folk had to say, and the fact that some of the members where friends of mine, and often times we would go and hang out after rehearsals and do things, which did not bother me any, because I sometimes dreaded going home to my significant other, who became a turn off to me. I remember CC saying to me, that the man I was seeing was my security blanket, and," yes", she was right, he was my security blanket, it was a blanket that I was able to hide underneath of not having to deal with going back home to live with my egg Donor, and not knowing how to go out on a limb, in order to live and survive on my own.

The trip I liked the most, was the trip to Detroit Michigan, and the hospitality that we received was phenomenal, this church paid for the choir, and the other members who came along to support our Pastor, to go and tour the Motown Museum. I must say it was a pleasure to see where history began, and the tourist guide happened to be Barry Gordy's sister, she did not at first acknowledge herself as being Mr. Gordy's sister, but of course there is always a big mouth out every bunch who don't know how to keep there mouths shut, and when he ever called her out in front of everyone, you could tell by the expressions on her face that she did not want everyone to know who she was, because if she did, I believe she would have told us in the beginning. I was amazed to see that this man started a business out of his own home, and too listen to the stories of how Michael Jackson (Rest In Peace), Stevie Wonder and Dianna Ross and the Supremes, and others were discovered. She said that Gordy Discovered Stevie outside playing his harmonica, this church also paid for us to go and eat at this all you can eat soul food restaurant, which was nasty as all hell, but it was the thought that count, and trust, and believe, that I was truly grateful. After that they took us on a tour in and around the areas of Detroit, and showed us land marks of important places, but the thing that caught my eye and others too, was the fact that they had so many houses, and buildings that was burnt, I could not believe all of what I was seeing, because there were lots of streets with burnt houses, and the towns looked as if they were deserted.

Eventually my significant other and I moved out of Randolph to Quincy Ma, and there is when I really started falling out of Love with him, and seeing the man that I had an interest in, and who attends one of the local churches in the South End of Boston, since I was sixteen years of age. This was truly a turning point of my life, because eventually my significant other found out about the affair that I was having.

WORDS OF ENCOURAGEMENT

Olive oil is symbolic of the Holy Spirit, you can't buy anointing, and until you go through, what I went through, you can't get what I got!

After you go through and suffer for a while, God will give you the glory!

There is nothing like purpose to deliver you from foolishness!

People get tied up in sin and foolishness, because they have nothing else to do!

When you are purpose driven, you don't have time for anything, because you are too busy working for God!

Nothing in life happens by accident, it's a sign when you belong to God, when He chastens you!

God anointed me to prophesize, and to minister through writing!

Find the will of God (John 7:17)

In the pursuit of Gods will, (Ephesians 5:17)

Be saved and win others, live Godly and Holy, be effective in giving of oneself into the lives of others!

The Lord in Mercy don't let you know everything, and that's where many of us fail, because we don't know how to wait and be still for God to answer the unknown, You have to have Faith, in knowing that God is going to work it out, not our will, but His will be done!
(Mathew 13:13-15)

You must be fully committed, and delight yourself in the Lord (2nd Chronicles, when Solomon asks for wisdom), and that means you will have to cut folk loose, so that God can began to mature you in who he has called you to be, everyone has been called, but only a few receive what their calling is, and others die, without knowing their purpose in God!

You must trust the purity of your heart! (Philippians 1:16, 2:13-14) (God rejects Saul for disobedience, 1st Samuel 13 chapter)

You must walk carefully through the door in order to walk circumspectly!
(Psalm 24:6 & Judges 6:7)

Note: when you are not sure if you are being lead by the Holy Spirit (when in doubt), ask questions; "Is this you Lord?" it might be the trick of the enemy too have you to do something that you don't have the gift to do!
(KNOWING YOUR CALLING)

Act in a presumptuous way, by asking God for confirmation!
(Confirmed means: to strengthen)

There are too many Pastors and Churches, who are just saving folks and not bringing them to the full maturity of Christ!
(Ephesians 5:15-21)

"GOD WILL USE WHO HE WANTS"

A lot of people, who are docile, slothful, lazy, fearful or intimidated, or insecure, have never really seen the anointing of God on their life.
The reason being is because they don't function!
("Conjunction junction, what's your function?")
The anointing is for someone who is going to do something, if you are not going to do anything, why would God anoint you to sit, or to look cute, to make excuses, to procrastinate, to sit back and lay back, and not do anything for Him!

People can hurt you in Church, but don't let Church hurt hold you back from your destiny, stay in the camp until you are healed, God will mend your broken heart, only if you stay, for this race was not given to the swift, neither to the strong, but to those who will endure it until the day of Jesus Christ!

"IF GOD IS BEFORE YOU, HE IS MORE GREATER THAN THE WORLD" THAT IS AGAINST
YOU,
BE BLESSED!
AND
LET YOU'RE WORDS COME OUT IN FRONT OF YOUR ENEMIES
BECAUSE GOD DID NOT GIVE US THE SPIRIT OF FEAR!

"I HAVE NOTHING TO FEAR, BUT FEAR ITSELF"

TIME BRINGS ABOUT A CHANGE

AND

ANYTHING THAT DOES NOT CHANGE IS DEFORMED

TEST THE SPIRIT, BY THE SPIRIT
BECAUSE EVERYONE
IS NOT FOR
YOU!

With Love,
Author, J'Korey Mills

Ps: Wondering why I did not die? I'll be happy to tell you why!

GOD FAVORED ME!